YOU WILL NOT BE REMEMBERED FOR THAT

RECEIVING GOD'S LOVE + LOVING YOURSELF + MOVING FORWARD

OLIVIA MOORE

Harrison House

Tulsa, OK

10 9 8 7 6 5 4 3 2 1   17 18 19 20

You Will Not Be Remembered for That
ISBN: 978-1-68031-138-9
Copyright © 2017 by Olivia Moore

Published by Harrison House Publishers
Tulsa, OK 74145
www.harrisonhouse.com

ENDORSEMENT

I have known this anointed woman since she was a child, growing up in her father's church, and I watched her mature into a fine young lady with a passion for God. I also witnessed her subsequent devastation and challenges. She was crushed but in her brokenness, she didn't quit. Instead, she cried out to God and she found the power to overcome every torment and lie of the enemy.

You Will Not Be Remembered For That is Olivia's story as she discovered that power in learning the depth of God's Love. Regardless of circumstances, or no matter the personal failures, she has come to understand the immensity of His unfailing Love. And that truth brought her out of the darkness and she KNOWS nothing can hinder her now from obtaining the "good life" God has prepared for her. His love leads to fulfillment, purpose, and joy!

Would you like to see your "story" change? Then, this is the book for you. God has ordained your life to be outstanding – to be a testimony to His Love and faithfulness. Meditate on the truths Olivia shares and get ready to enjoy life better than you've ever imagined!

Dr. Jerry Savelle
Jerry Savelle Ministries International

CONTENTS

Conclusion: What Will You Be Remembered For?

SPECIAL THANKS AND SINCEREST GRATITUDE

First and foremost, to my Father God, thank you for loving me unconditionally and choosing me as your very own Daughter; You are my joy and my life. With all of my heart, I am eternally grateful and humbled to have been given the honor of being entrusted with this message. Thank you for every life that will be touched by your love and words of freedom. I give you every ounce of the glory because it is all only by You. You are the real author of this book and the One who brought it to pass. Thank you, Jesus, for causing this message to become alive and to burn like a fire within the readers, stirring their hearts with the joy and vision of the great plans you have for them, for they are loved!

To my precious parents, Stan and Teresa Moore — Daddy, thank you for loving me no matter what and for showing me my entire life how Father God loves us. Mommy, thank you for being the biggest encourager in my life. You have always believed in me and you taught me to believe in myself. This book would not be in existence if it were not for the two of you. You both mean the world to me and each time I look at you, with a big smile, I think "Wow, they are my parents!" You are strength, refreshment, and joy to all who know you and I am honored to be your daughter. Thank you for loving me the way you do. I believe in you with my whole heart and I love you forever.

To my sister Victoria, my brother Stanley, sister-in-love Emily, and all of my family and friends, each one of you are irreplaceable and have contributed something vital and special to my life that I am forever grateful for. Your constant love, inspiration, and support have shaped my entire life. Thank you for being the best friends a girl could ever ask for. I love you.

To Esther Gualtieri, thank you for fearlessly pulling out the gold in others. My heart is so full thinking about the beautiful part you played to not only encourage me when I needed it the most, but also each life that God will touch through the message you helped to inspire and bring to light. With all of my heart, thank you for your obedience and encouragement. Keep loving like you do — your life is making such a lasting difference!

To Terri Savelle Foy, thank you for being beautiful you and for living your life to inspire others. I could never fully express how much you mean to me and how much I love you. The teachings God has given you literally saved my life and was the very thing that kept me going. You taught me to dream again and you made me see it was possible to do what always seemed impossible. Because of you, people are rising up to make their dreams bigger than their memories. Thank you for changing the world, like you have changed my life, by cheering us on to go after our dreams. Your love and support have made the difference.

To Cindy Kimbrough, you are a God-gifted editor and such a beautiful person. Thank you for your loving encouragement throughout the editing process. You are a blessing!

To Harrison House Publishers and the amazing, talented team of people there, thank you for making it possible for this message to get into the hands and hearts of people whose lives will forever be marked and defined by God's unchanging love and purpose for them. I am forever grateful for all of your love, hard work, and dedication. Thank you for giving me the opportunity and the great honor of working with you; you are so excellent at what you do and I am beyond grateful to have worked together on this project that is so dear to my heart.

And finally to YOU! With all of my heart, thank you for picking up this book. I believe it's not by coincidence, but a divine appointment set up by God and I am just so grateful and honored to go on this journey of freedom together. You are the very reason this book was written. I pray that God uses the words on these pages to pour out His love on you in a fresh, real, and personal way and to be the very thing to catapult you into your destiny. He is doing a new thing in your life and it starts now! Get ready, the best is yet to come. I love you and I believe in you. You are loved, you can love yourself, and you can move forward because YOU will not be remembered for that!

FOREWORD

You Will Not Be Remembered For That was written through first-hand experience of how much God cares about every detail of our lives — where you've been and where you're going. God loves you so much. He doesn't want one day, one month, one year of your life wasted in regrets, hurts, insecurities, and fears from the past.

Olivia will show you that your past does not define your future. She will lead you out of your past and into the unique vision and dreams God has for your life. You will never leave where you are until you decide where you'd rather be. It's time to make your dreams bigger than your memories!

I know what it's like to have memories bigger than my dreams; to spend more time thinking about my past than thinking about my future. I understand what it feels like to be tormented by the past and to think, "I've blown it, I've made too many mistakes. It's too late for me. I've missed out on the plan of God for my life." It's even worse to not even know His plan and just be existing, doing the same thing year after year.

Yet, I also know what it's like to finally discover a dream or a goal. There is something God wants you to do during your time on this earth, not just existing back there in the past. I thank the Lord that I finally discovered how to be free and now have the privilege of cheering others on and leading them into a life of purpose.

It blesses my heart to see how the message the Lord has given me gave Olivia the strength to move forward and now strengthen others to do the same. Our families have been divinely connected for years and I am so happy to see how that has blossomed into our precious relationship.

While we were in Paris together on a ministry trip, Olivia shared the vision for this book and her desire to help others live free from the shame of their past. My heart was immediately touched by this message because I know that there are so many who want to move on but something is still keeping them back, something still has a hold on them and like a rope, it is pulling them back, away from the plan of God for their lives.

Years ago, I was at a Believers' Convention in Anaheim, California. I was sitting on the second row, when Reverend Oral Roberts was escorted in and seated on the front row, directly in front of me.

All of a sudden he looked me square in the eyes, pointed at me and said, "There's something you're not letting go of! Lift your hands."

I raised both hands and in front of TV cameras and thousands of people, he started hitting the bottom of my elbows and repeated, "Let go! Let go! Let go!"

To tell you the truth, I was oblivious to what I could be holding on to. It wasn't until I flew back home to Texas and was out walking one morning that the Lord suddenly spoke to me inside my spirit and gave me the answer.

He said, "It's the shame of your past, Terri. It's time to let it go."

I didn't realize that I was still carrying so much inside. I was allowing my past to define me. I was holding on to so many regrets, so many mistakes, things I wished I could just press delete on and pretend never happened. I was holding on to all of that for years and letting it mold who I thought I was.

Only months after that experience, I heard Pastor Mac Hammond say that "shame and guilt will keep you from your calling." In other words, you will never do what God has called to do if you are holding on to the shame and guilt of your past.

Satan has traps set up to keep you back. That is why Philippians 3:13 (KJV) says, "...but this one thing I do, forgetting those things which are behind, and reaching forth unto those things which are before." Forgetting and reaching; let go of the past but hang on to the future.

It's not your past that keeps you from God's best; it's your remembrance of it. God says in Isaiah 43:18 (NLT), "But forget all that — it is nothing compared to what I am going to do." Whatever that means for you, God desires for you to move past your past so He can do a new thing in your life and now it shall spring forth. You may be crying out for a fresh start, but God can't do a new thing if you are still holding on to the old thing.

What do you need to let go of? Memories of your past may be assaulting your mind, trying to change your perception of who God says you are. The invaluable wisdom that Olivia shares will help you let go of that baggage and to see yourself as free and clean, just how God sees you.

I wholeheartedly believe in this message and I want to congratulate you on your pursuit of feeding on truth and overriding Satan's lies. Only you can choose to receive the love that God has for you; only you can forgive yourself; only you can choose to take the next step to move forward. The fact that you have picked up this book proves that you are ready to give your past a burial and move into the plan of God for your life, so get ready to imagine big and live a life freer than you ever thought possible!

My prayer is that this book may be your defining moment with just you and God where you once and for all, let it go. Everything God has for you is ahead of you. From this day forward, make your dreams far bigger than the memories of your past, knowing that You Will Not Be Remembered For That!

Terri Savelle Foy
Motivator and Success Coach

INTRODUCTION

I awoke to another morning on the other side of the world, smack dab in the middle of a missions trip. With my eyes barely open, I received a text message from a precious friend. She gave details about a dream she'd recently had and as she did, I imagined it vividly:

The sun was slowly setting as a cool, summer breeze filled the night air. The two of us were enjoying a relaxing walk down the street when, from out of nowhere, a man we did not know came up and started describing in perfect detail a time in my life of which I was very ashamed. The man vividly rehearsed exact words I had spoken and instances that had taken place, things no other person on the face of the planet knew about. He knew that I had gone through a divorce and hadn't been fully the same since. He knew how much pain I'd been through due to the choices I made and how I had considered taking my own life.

He also knew my opinion of myself had been shattered, and that I now viewed myself as damaged goods, forever tainted by that one moment in time. He accurately described my struggle to move forward because I was chained to the past by my shame and regret.

I stood there, wide-eyed and speechless, wondering how in the world this man whom I'd never met before, could know all of this. I felt so confused. Just when I thought I would burst into tears, the man moved closer, looked me straight in the eye and said, "She will not be remembered for that." His voice conveyed both undeniable authority and boundless compassion: "She will not be remembered for that."

The words continued to ring out, increasing in volume until they thundered down the street, "She will not be remembered for that! SHE WILL NOT BE REMEMBERED FOR THAT!"

I was shocked and captivated by my friend's message and continued to read it over and over. I could not have received that text message at a more perfect time.

I'd been ashamed of so much, of shocking things that had happened in my past, of situations I'd never imagined I would have encountered. My experiences had left me shattered. Though time had passed, healing had taken place and much personal progress had been made, there were still many days when I felt stuck. I battled feelings of loneliness and fear and just couldn't see how my life would ever be the same again.

Overwhelmed with shame and guilt, I hated who I had become and could not find a way to forgive myself. I began to believe that I was no longer qualified to be a part of anything significant and was convinced my life's purpose was lost. I would become obsessed with trying to figure out what people must be thinking about me now, or, if they even thought of me at all. I was afraid that my life had been forever tainted by the mistakes and wrong decisions I had made. I felt trapped in a vicious cycle of taking 10 steps forward, only to have someone say something or a painful memory flash before my eyes that would pull me 15 steps back into the quicksand of my past.

But reading the words of this text from my friend, I was deeply moved. I fell to my knees, buried my face in my hands and cried out to God. I began to thank Him for His amazing love for me and His great, unending grace. As I closed my eyes, I pictured Jesus standing there, looking at me with compassion and I was enveloped in the waves of love that radiated from who He is.

With no hint of regret, He shouted, "She will not be remembered for that!" He did not whisper the words; His voice held no trace of shame or hesitation. With boldness, righteous authority, power and dominance, He deprived condemnation of its power, shaking the past out of me.

"SHE WILL NOT BE REMEMBERED FOR THAT!"

"SHE WILL NOT BE REMEMBERED FOR THAT!"

"SHE WILL NOT BE REMEMBERED FOR THAT!"

Those words exploded in my spirit. I couldn't stop crying. As I continued to picture Jesus speaking those words of life and freedom to me, He washed away the memory and pain of my past, filling me with His peace and love.

I was finally free to receive God's amazing love. My eyes were opened to the truth that when God thinks about me, He does not think about everything I have done wrong. He does not remember me by what I have done or haven't done. He simply sees me and He loves me.

This realization empowered and refreshed me. I realized that since God is not ashamed of me and does not see me as tainted, I do not need to view myself that way. God does not look at me as damaged goods, so I should not go on treating myself that way. I was finally truly able to forgive myself.

I realized that I must not remember myself by my past or view myself through the lens of my failures because I am not defined by what lies behind. The things I had gone through were all temporal. There was far more to me and the rest of my life than the mistakes I had made in my past. My life and my future would not be defined by any one moment in time.

Within that beautiful moment, I began to speak over myself those same words I pictured Jesus saying. With tears streaming down my face, I declared, "I will not be remembered for that!"

The more I said it, the more real it became to me. I was empowered to move forward. I realized that there was more for me to do with my life. The chains of my past and the limitations I had put on myself were falling off as Jesus made all things new.

I will not be remembered for that!

I will not be remembered for that!

As I took my eyes off my past, I was able to recognize there were still people for me to reach, nations for me to love, and dreams to be fulfilled. God still wanted to use me. I was empowered to move forward; the strings that once tied me to my past were finally broken. The mental strongholds that had kept me stuck in my old rut of shame were deprived of their power. There was more of my life to be lived and I finally was determined to live it! My eyes were now focused on knowing God more each day and on helping other people. I was flooded with a fresh desire to have my life be remembered for these things.

I believe that the message of that dream is not just for me. It used to be very difficult for me to share personal things with other people, especially things of which I have been ashamed. However, God has laid this book upon my heart because I know that He wants you to realize how precious you are to Him and how much He loves you. He doesn't want you to live another day bound to your past. He doesn't want you to go another hour not truly liking yourself or viewing yourself as subpar because of mistakes you have made or things that have happened to you.

God loves you and He wants you to love yourself. You are beautiful. You are priceless. You are irreplaceable. The blood of Jesus was shed just for you so you can be made completely new. Jesus is not ashamed of you! He has personally taken away your past and He wants you to live a life that is fresh and new, with your shoulders back and head lifted high, knowing that nothing can derail the marvelous plans He has for your life!

If sharing my personal experiences and what God has shown me through His Word can help you in any way, I want to do it. That is the purpose of this book. Dear friend, although we may not ever meet face to face, I want you to know that God loves you and so do I. I believe in you. No matter what you are going through, please know that this is not the end. Don't give up. God is doing a new thing in your life and your best days are ahead of you. I know what it's like to feel stuck, to want to move forward but to feel like something is holding you back. I know what it's like to be overwhelmed with shame and guilt. However, in His great love, Jesus has changed everything!

He saved my life from the pit of destruction and has restored my soul. Jesus has changed how I view myself, He has empowered me to move forward and He wants to do the very same thing for you! It is time for you to live each day with the confidence that you are not defined by what lies behind. There is far more to who you are than what you have gone through in the past. You are not your mistakes. You are not your failures. No matter what you have done or haven't done, no matter where you have been, what you have gone through, or what people may have done to you – your Father God loves you dearly. You are the child He always wanted.

God wants to take what has been ruined in your life, touch it by His grace, and turn it into something more beautiful than you could ever imagine. He will give you beauty for ashes, the oil of joy for mourning, and the garment of praise for the spirit of heaviness as He completely heals your heart and restores your soul (Isaiah 61:3). He desires to take the moments in your life that have caused you so much shame and turn them around for your good, using them as a catalyst to propel you into a future that is full of hope!

God loves you with an unchanging and unfailing love and He believes in you. Your Father God is so much greater than your past; He has the power to restore your life in unthought of and unexpected ways. He is unashamed to call you His very own, as He has handcrafted you for greatness. Jesus has set you free to move forward.

When the years pass by and all is said and done, you can know that you have run your race with great joy and accomplished all that God called you to do. Those negative experiences in your life that have tried to keep you bound, that seemed so massive, will one day never be thought of. Those things will be nothing but examples of what God turned around and worked for your good. This is not the end. Your life is far from over. That moment in your past does not have to dictate or define your future. Your life has far greater meaning and purpose than your mistakes.

Thank you for going on this journey with me. I am so excited about all that God is doing in your life! Get ready to live with a freedom and joy that you never knew existed. I pray that as you read, the Spirit of God will make the Father's love real to you, turn on the light to show you who you already are in Christ, and ignite a fresh passion within your heart to leave the past in the past and run the race that is set before you. God loves you with an unchanging, unfailing love and He believes in you. It is time to love yourself. It is time to let go of the things that are behind you and move forward with freshness and confidence, knowing that God is turning the tide in your life!

All out of love, Jesus came to set the captive free. The prison door has been flung open wide and you do not have to live one more moment of your life as a prisoner of your past. Today is a new day. God, in His unending love, is doing a new thing in your life; it has already begun! God is for you. How can you lose with God on your side? He is holding out your fresh start and declaring that it is time to go forward! Dream new dreams. Shake off the dust of the past, arise and shine because He has a future that is full of hope, just waiting for you.

Hear the bold shout of triumph and take it for yourself. Jesus, your glory and the lifter of your head, is calling you to live free from all shame, knowing that YOU WILL NOT BE REMEMBERED FOR THAT!

With love,

Olivia

PART ONE

Receiving
God's Love

CHAPTER 1

JESUS LOVES YOU — BELIEVE IT!

I was babysitting two of my favorite little boys. After a non-stop, eventful day of riding bikes, playing basketball, and baking cookies, it was time for bed. I tucked the kiddos in, and five-year-old John cuddled by my side. As the peaceful quiet of night filled the room, I read him his bedtime story.

His little eyes were barely open and his head was sinking deep into his pillow, when all of a sudden he tenderly whispered three simple words: "Jesus loves you." My heart melted immediately. Enamored, I said "Aww. Thank you, John. Jesus loves you, too." I paused for a moment, smiled, then continued on with the story.

Just a few seconds passed when he unexpectedly repeated the words in his innocent voice, "Jesus loves you."

Smiling ear to ear, I replied, "That's so sweet, John. Thank you."

We'd only made it to page three when again John whispered, "Jesus loves you."

Again I said, "Aww, thank you." Back and forth we went, and after five or six exchanges, it finally hit me. The most powerful and life-changing words a person could ever hear were coming straight out of a five-year-old boy's mouth.

I was raised in a Christian household. My parents and grand-parents are pastors of a vibrant church, and I started preaching when I was 15 years old. Although I had literally heard that simple truth my entire life, that night in that little bunk bed, something changed on the inside of me. It was like I was hearing those words for the very first time. I was fresh out of a divorce, babysitting, trying to figure out where my life would go from there and, in the midst of it all, a five-year-old was telling me Jesus loves me.

I wanted to cry. I wanted to shout. I wanted to laugh. Jesus loves me — could it truly be? Even after I had acted so unimaginably ugly and made so many wrong decisions? Even though I hated who I believed I had become as I looked at myself through the lens of my failures? Even though others had a negative opinion of me? I was convinced I was damaged goods, forever tainted by that one moment in time. I had even been on the verge of taking my own life; I felt stuck in a dark pit, not knowing how my life would ever be the same again. I had done so much wrong and experienced immense shame, hopelessness, and pain. But guess what? None of that had changed a single thing. Jesus still loved me!

Right there in that wooden bunk bed, my heart was flooded with light personally knowing that, without a doubt, Jesus loved me and God had a wonderful plan of victory for my life. There is nothing like the love of God to kick open the floodgates of joy and radically illuminate a person with the assurance that somehow, God is going to turn their circumstances around for their good!

Get ready for the best part. Those same, three powerful words apply to you: Jesus loves *you*. If He loves and believes in anybody, trust me, it's you. Let that simple yet massive truth take root in your heart. The same way Jesus loves me is the same way He loves every person on the face of the planet, and His love is unending, unconditional, and unchanging. Jesus loves you. Did you get that? Jesus loves you; yes, *you*!

If you are like me and have heard that your entire life, right now, allow your heart to hear it as if it were the very first time: Jesus loves you. These three words contain the power to transform your life if you will let them. And if you have never heard those words before, let me be the first to say them to you: Jesus loves you. At this very moment, you can choose to let the power of His limitless love set your soul free. He loves you with everything He is. After everything you have or haven't done and all the mistakes you have made, even smack dab in the middle of that huge mess you are facing right now, He still loves you and has a purpose for your life.

Jesus knows the moments that have brought you so much pain and caused you to become disappointed in yourself. Right there, even if you're within the walls of that prison cell or on the floor of that dark bathroom where you're hopelessly turning to drugs, know this: Jesus loves you. We can never hear that too many times. Jesus loves you, and He always will. He loves you individually. He loves you specifically. God is for you and He believes in you. He paid the highest price imaginable to do what you could never do — rescue yourself from that pit of despair. God wants to take the very thing the devil meant to destroy and by His grace, turn it around for your good! Jesus wants to exchange your past for a future full of hope. The good life of victory has your name on it!

What glorious freedom is found in the truth that you are forever loved. Yet, it is one thing to hear that phrase and say you know it and a completely different thing to go beyond just knowing to the point that you deposit all your trust and all of who you are upon the foundation of God's unchanging love. First John 4:16 says, "And we know (understand, recognize, are conscious of, by observation and by experience) and believe (adhere to and put faith in and rely on) the love God cherishes for us." When you become convinced God loves you individually and that He is on your side, His love will become so alive to you that it will define who you are. His love has the power to remove all shame and give definition to your life if you are willing to go one step beyond knowing and choose to believe. Be careful not to fall into the trap of thinking that you believe something just because you have heard it for so long. Familiarity and belief are not the same thing.

You must not allow what other people say and your own self-perception to foster the hidden belief that says, "Of course God loves a good person like you, but He does not really care about me; I've messed up way too much." Perhaps you have always had a picture of God upset, mad, or frustrated with you. Maybe you feel like a worthless failure and find it difficult to love yourself, so you have no reason to believe anyone else could. Maybe no one has ever told you they love you, or perhaps the people who said they did are nowhere to be found.

No matter where you are today and no matter what you have gone through, hear this with your whole heart: God loves you with everything He is, and that love will never go away. Rest knowing that His love isn't like the "love" of this world, based on performance or behavior. He doesn't say He loves you and then walk out a week later. He isn't going anywhere; He always has loved you and always will.

Gifts Are Free

Imagine a child on Christmas morning, darting down the staircase, enthralled by the glistening Christmas tree. The little girl's jaw drops and her eyes become as big as saucers, captivated by a brand new, shiny pink bike with a giant, glittery bow on it. The little girl jumps on her bike, squeals with excitement and then dashes over to her parents to thank them with hugs and kisses. But then her parents sit her down and say, "Now sweetie, I know it's Christmas, but in order for you to ride your bike, you'll need to work eight hours a day for the next five years, cleaning the house." What a disappointing Christmas that would be!

A gift is not a gift if we work for it. The fact that someone else pays for it is part of what makes it a gift. It is given out of grace, not based on anything you did to attain it. When you receive your regular paycheck every week, you don't go up to your boss and say, "Wow, thank you for thinking of me and giving me this check. What a huge surprise!" No, you earned it, you worked for it; a paycheck is something you deserve. However, one of the most important things about God's love is that we could never earn it, and we could never deserve it. Unlike a paycheck, God's love is not owed to you. You could try your entire life, but I promise you, you could never do enough good to earn His love. God's love is a gift, something He freely gives to all, purely out of grace. It is never based on our good works.

Choose to speak words that magnify God's love in your life. Especially when you feel like you least deserve His love, put your focus on it and thank Him for His free grace. Your words control your quality of life. If you don't like the direction your life is headed, grab a hold of the steering wheel and change your course by changing your words. The Bible makes it clear that life and death are in the power of the tongue and you can choose to speak life. God will change your life if you will change what you're saying.

Speaking this way will take you beyond just knowing or hearing about God's love, to believing that His love is unchanging and unending and then, to receiving it for yourself. God wants you to take His love for yourself and believe that no matter what, the precious blood of Jesus is more powerful than your past because His love is stronger than your sins. He is for you and He is on your side.

When a friend sends a package to my home and I receive it, I let them know the gift has arrived by telling them thank you. Giving thanks confirms I have received the gift and am grateful for it. In the same way, I show God that I have received His free gift of love by giving Him thanks for it. Now, if a friend told me ahead of time that they sent a gift to me, I would not wait until I actually saw the gift and held it in my hands before I thanked them. No, if I believed what they told me, I would open up my mouth and thank them for the gift even before I received it. Right now, before you see any reason to, if you will give God thanks, your gratitude will release great power into your life.

The Gift Giver

God will get into your life however He can, wherever He sees an open door, just like He did with me that night I was babysitting. Out of the mouth of a little five year old, the truth that Jesus loves me ignited a fresh hope and new life on the inside of me. That night, I went beyond just knowing about God's love and I chose to believe it. His love is the very fuel that gives meaning to your life and your words are the booster cables that will ignite that spark, causing His love to be a living reality to you.

I left little John's bunk bed dancing. My eyes were flooded with the light of what God said and I realized it didn't matter where I had been or what I had done, His love would never go away! God loves us with an unchanging, unfailing love. His love is not based on what we have done. We can never be so good we earn more of His affection, and we can't be so bad He loves us any less. Nothing, absolutely nothing, has the power to erase the love that He has for you.

> So, what do you think? With God on our side like this, how can we lose? If God didn't hesitate to put everything on the line for us, embracing our condition and exposing himself to the worst by sending his own Son, is there anything else he wouldn't gladly and freely do for us? And who would dare tangle with God by messing with one of God's chosen? Who would dare even to point a finger? The one who died for us — who was raised to life for us — is in the presence of God at this very moment sticking up for us. Do you think anything can drive a wedge between us and Christ's love? No! Not trouble, not hard times, not hatred, not hunger, not home-lessness, not bullying threats, not backstabbing, not even the worst sins listed in Scripture:
>
> None of this fazes us because Jesus loves us. I'm absolutely convinced that nothing—nothing living or dead, angelic or demonic, today or tomorrow, high or low, thinkable or unthinkable—absolutely nothing can get between us and God's love because of the way that Jesus our Master has embraced us.
>
> ### Romans 8:31–39 (MSG)

Isn't that passage amazing? Jesus is not pointing His finger at you. God is not sitting in heaven waiting to beat you down over your mistakes. There is no condemnation in Jesus, only perfect freedom! God has already demonstrated His love for you in the most extravagant way possible, by sending His very own Son, Jesus Christ, to die for you and raising Him from the dead. Jesus endured the cross and conquered hell, death, and the grave all for you! There is absolutely nothing else He would hesitate to do for you. Everything you will ever need is in Jesus. God loves you and He is on your side. Let His love define who you are, and when a seemingly impossible situation tries to back you into a corner, look it square in its eyes and ask, "How can I lose? God is on my side!" Nothing has to shake you; your past no longer has to intimidate you. Jesus loves you and there is no fear in His love.

When we give our lives to Jesus, He comes to live inside of our hearts by His Spirit. The Bible tells us in 1 John 4:8 that God is love. Thus, Love Himself comes to live on the inside of us forever and He will never leave us. Hebrews 13:5 says, "For He [God] Himself has said, I will not in any way fail you nor give you up nor leave you without support. [I will] not, [I will] not, [I will] not in any degree leave you helpless nor forsake nor let [you] down (relax My hold on you)! [Assuredly not!]" (AMP). Don't you just love that!?

Realize Who is talking to you right now — HE, GOD HIM-SELF! The creator of heaven and earth. The one who always was and always will be. God is looking directly at you, telling you not just once, but reassuring your heart by saying it three times, "I will not, I will not, I will not in ANY degree leave you!" He will never leave you or give up on you in any way or any day. The Message Bible puts it this way: "God assured us, 'I'll never let you down, never walk off and leave you.'" That is good news! Even when you fail over and over again, God is never going to leave the scene and walk off. Your sin does not intimidate Him, and your mistakes do not take away a single ounce of His love.

Choose to Believe and Receive

Today can be a fresh start where you go beyond just hearing about the possibility of being loved and choose to believe that God loves you with everything that He is. You can live with a freedom you didn't know existed, consumed with a joy you didn't know was possible. God is love and you are forever wanted and chosen by Him.

Choosing to believe what God says about you and living in the freedom He has given takes an act of your will. It requires you actively choosing to receive His love every day. His love is always right there, but it will not be a reality until you receive it for yourself. Imagine someone has purchased a special gift and delivered it right to your doorstep. Even though the gift is right there waiting for you, you cannot enjoy it until you open it up. In the same way, God's love for you is more real than anything else in this world. His love has your name on it and it is constantly knocking on your door. However, you must receive it if you want to experience that love personally.

According to 2 Corinthians 4:13, we "believe and therefore we speak." In other words, if you truly believe something, you speak it out loud. The reverse is also true; if you want to believe something more, speak it. The more you hear your own voice say it, the more you will begin to believe it. Believing gives way to receiving.

Our words are like a magnifying glass; they have the power to make things bigger in our lives. Our words are also like a magnet; they attract things to us. What you talk about will become more real to you. Your words draw those things to your life. Let me encourage you to speak about God's love, no matter where you are in life. Begin talking to yourself about how much God loves you. Whether you feel like it or not, show God you trust Him. Thank Him that His love is more real to you than anything else in your life. Speak that over and over. Right now, simply tell Him out loud, "Father God, thank You for loving me with such a great love. I know exactly who I am — I am loved! I believe and I receive Your love for me."

Before you see or feel it, declare God's love is more real than anything else in your life. This will allow that truth to take root and illuminate your heart with faith. This is what faith is all about! We walk by faith and not by sight. We do not live according to what we see and feel, we live according to what we believe! But remember, faith without works is dead. There is always evidence to faith and the biggest evidence of your faith is speaking out what you believe. This is how overcomers live. This is how happy, victorious children of God choose to live.

Trust me, I know what it is like to live as a perfectionist, demanding perfection from myself and all of those around me. But God is not that way! He is not looking for perfect people. He is just looking for someone to trust Him enough to allow His love to transform their life.

God wants you to come to Him unhindered by what lies behind you. Throw your past before His feet and run into His arms that are always wide open, just waiting for you. God is not mad at you and He certainly is not holding anything against you. All because of love, Jesus died on the cross to take away your sins and failures. God raised Him from the dead to proclaim the Good News that when you believe on Jesus and the power of His life-giving, cleansing blood, from that moment on when God looks at you, He does not see what you did ten years ago or what you did even last night. Rather, He chooses to see the price that was paid for you and He sees the real you. You are not your sin, you are not your failures, and you are not what other people have done to you. You are the beautiful child He has always wanted and the one He calls His very own.

Bank all of your trust and all of who you are upon that love. You are not defined by what you do or by what other people think about you. None of that gives you your value. Your value comes from one place — Jesus. When you fully rely on His unchanging love, your confidence will no longer be on what you look like or what you accomplish. As the roots of your being go down deep in Jesus and you experience the breadth, depth, and height of His endless love, shame and intimidation are deprived of their power. In their place will stand an unshakable confidence. There will be such a fearlessness about you, a boldness that comes from knowing your Heavenly Father.

CHAPTER 2

CHOSEN

John 15:16 says, "You have not chosen me, but I have chosen you and I have appointed and placed and purposefully planted you." And Ephesians 1:4 says, "Even as [in His love] He chose us [actually picked us out for Himself as His own] in Christ before the foundation of the world, that we should be holy (consecrated and set apart for Him) and blameless in His sight, even above reproach, before Him in love."

These verses tell us that before the foundations of the world, God thought about you and it made Him happy. Before this planet took shape, before the oceans and the mountains were formed, before any humans or animals walked on the face of the earth, you — yes *you* — were alive in the heart of God. Without hesitation, the author of time and architect of heavens and earth fell in love with you. The moment you first entered His thoughts, He knew this world would not be complete without you. He smiled at the dream of you. You danced in His imagination and flourished in His thoughts.

He is your Creator. He handcrafted your smile. He meticulously designed every detail of your personality. With tenderness and care, He deposited passions and abilities within your heart. He breathed His life into your being. He counted down the days till your birth; He has written down your days in a book. He was there when you took your first breath and gave your first cry. You are God's dream come true. You are His work of art and irreplaceable in His heart. You are the child He has always wanted.

Never believe the lies that you are a mistake or that you never should have been born. Never allow thoughts that nobody cares about you or wants you to creep into your mind. You are not an accident. You are not a mistake. You may have made mistakes, but please let me reassure you, you are NOT a mistake. Others may have told you everyone would have been better off without you, but that is a lie straight from the pit of hell. This world would *not* be better off without you. God knew exactly what He was doing! God wanted you in His family.

Handpicked for the Winning Team

When I was in fifth grade, kickball was the highlight of each school day and every kid counted down the hours until recess. There would always be two teams and each captain would go back and forth, carefully scanning all of the kids, hunting for the top players. One by one, they would call out the names of those they desired to be on their team. Anxiously waiting within the crowd, I always wanted to be the kid who was chosen first. The moment I heard my name, something would inevitably sweep over me and I would walk out on the court with such confidence. With my shoulders back and head held high, I felt on top of the world. There is an undeniable difference in our attitude, posture, and self-perception when we know we were chosen and not just stuck with someone by default.

In any sport, a player's status is constantly changing based on his or her performance. Their value is determined by their actions, which means their worth is constantly on the verge of fluctuation. But it is not that way with God. We are God's very first choice every single time. He handpicked us out of the crowd and said, "That's the one I want. I choose her." This truth that we are chosen, that we are wanted, means that we can go out on the court of life and face each day with confidence, knowing we are loved.

It is good news to be chosen! There is so much joy in knowing you are not merely tolerated, but deeply wanted and daily celebrated by God. Believe me, His love for you can never be exhausted. He handpicked you out of the crowd and He created you on purpose for a purpose.

God Won't Change His Mind

In the heart of God, our status does not change based on our performance. Our worth will never fluctuate because it has no correlation to our performance. No matter what mistakes we have made or what other people have said or done, God will always choose us. There is nothing — not one thing —we could ever do to make God love us any more than He already does. Equally important, there is nothing we could ever do that could make God love us any less.

Romans 11:29 says, "For God's gifts and His calls are irrevocable. [He never withdraws them when once they are given, and He does not change His mind about those to whom He gives His grace or to whom He sends His call]" (AMP). Let this truth saturate your very being and become part of the fabric of who you are. God will never, no never, change His mind about you!

Your actions and mistakes may change someone else's opinion of you, but nothing that you do has the power to change God's opinion of you. Even if you are disappointed in yourself, realize that your negative self-perception does not reflect how God thinks. He is not one bit mad at you. Let me reassure you, God made up His mind about you a long time ago! The Bible tells us that God picked you out for Himself and planned in love for you before the foundations of the world. He loved you before you had the slightest chance to earn His affection. He chose to love you with all that He is. It is because of this endless love that God sent Jesus to die on the cross for you.

> "For God so [greatly] loved and dearly prized the world, that He [even] gave His [One and] only begotten Son, so that whoever believes and trusts in Him [as Savior] shall not perish, but have eternal life. 17 For God did not send the Son into the world to judge and condemn the world [that is, to initiate the final judgment of the world], but that the world might be saved through Him.
>
> John 3:16–17 (AMP)

God gave everything He had just to get you. You are precious to Him and you are constantly on His mind. He had to have you. Do not listen to the lies that you are worthless, the God of the universe paid the highest price imaginable for you. Jesus did not want to go on living without you, that is why He died to get you. God greatly loves and prizes you. Jesus conquered hell, death, and the grave, and you were His grand prize! He put Satan under your feet so that you could live free in His marvelous love and belong to Him forever.

The Value of One

In Luke chapter 15, Jesus told a story about a shepherd who had 100 sheep. When just one of them wandered away, he left the 99 others to go after the one until he found it. He refused to quit until that precious little sheep was back in his arms. The moment the man found his beloved sheep, great joy swept his heart as he placed it on his shoulders.

In that same chapter, Jesus also described a woman who owned 10 silver coins. When she misplaced just one, she turned the whole house upside down, frantically searching for the lost coin, refusing to give up no matter how long it took. The woman was so thrilled when she finally found her coin that she told her friends what had happened so that they could rejoice with her.

Even though you're just one person, you matter to God. You are worth far more than rubies and gold. You are known and noticed by the God of the whole universe, and the King of Kings gave His life to purchase your freedom. You are not just another face in the crowd. You are not forgotten in a sea of people. God chose you in the very beginning, He created you, and He never stops thinking about you.

Yet, He did not stop there. Every other religion is about man trying to get to God; the emphasis is on man being judged by his deeds. The beautiful thing about Jesus is that He came to us! He is called Emmanuel, which means "God with us!" You may just be one, but you are the very one God loves and cherishes with all that He is.

John 3:18 says that there is no rejection or condemnation for those who believe in Jesus. Whosoever calls upon His Name shall be saved! All out of pure love, Jesus went beyond every boundary, He willingly stripped Himself of every heavenly privilege, became a servant, and carried His obedience to the extreme of death. You are the reason Jesus came.

While we were yet in weakness [powerless to help ourselves], at the fitting time Christ died for (in behalf of) the ungodly. Now it is an extraordinary thing for one to give his life even

for an upright man, though perhaps for a noble and lovable and generous benefactor someone might even dare to die. But God shows and clearly proves His [own] love for us by the fact that while we were still sinners, Christ (the Messiah, the Anointed One) died for us.

Romans 5:6–8

Jesus loved us at our darkest moment. He did what we could never do for ourselves. We were powerless to help ourselves, but our beautiful Savior rescued us from a life of bondage and shame. We were against Him, yet He freely laid down His life and died on the cross. What amazing love! Such a love is foreign to this world, but it is the very essence of who God is. His love is a free gift to us, but it is something for which He paid the highest price.

Not only does Jesus save us from spending eternity in hell, but He wants to save us from a life of torment here on the earth. He came that we might experience heaven on earth. On the foundation of His relentless love, God said, "I know what I'm doing. I have it all planned out—plans to take care of you, not abandon you, plans to give you the future you hope for" (Jeremiah 29:11 MSG). God has an amazing plan for your life and He always does above and beyond anything that we could hope, dream, or dare to imagine. He will turn things around in your life and cause you to always triumph. His love is a gift that He takes tremendous joy in giving and He is flooded with even more inexpressible joy when He sees you go on to believe, receive, and enjoy the freedom of that love each day. Remember, God chose you and He does not regret His choice!

CHAPTER 3

"THIS IS MY CHILD!"

In Luke 15, Jesus told a story about a guy who thought he had to be perfect to have value. He was fully convinced he had to earn his father's love, and that his worth fluctuated based on his actions. Let me give you the "Olivia Paraphrase" of what happened.

The story begins with a wealthy man who had two sons. One day, the younger son asked his father for his portion of the inheritance, which was basically his way of telling his dad, "I don't really care about you anymore. All I really care about is getting your money so I can go off and do whatever I want." With his inheritance in hand, the son went far away, seeking his own adventure. We don't know exactly what he did during this time in his life, but Jesus did say the son wasted his fortune in "reckless and loose [from restraint] living" (v. 13).

Perhaps hidden insecurities drove him to hide behind his newfound wealth and attempt to buy friends. Maybe past failures made him feel he was not a "real man" unless he was sleeping around with different women. Perhaps there was such an unshakeable void in the center of who he was that all he knew to do was cover up his emptiness with partying, alcohol, or gambling, money, or anything else he could get his hands on He was undeniably on a search to feel valuable. Yet, try as he might, he only ended up digging himself deeper into a pit of despair. These fleeting, external things didn't satisfy what was bothering him internally.

He invested all of his energy, time, and resources into trying to create this seemingly perfect life. He had a picture in his head of who he wanted to be and what he wanted his life to look like — happy, successful and popular. He was convinced that his happiness was linked to attaining the "next" thing. The saddest part is he was so unhappy, he felt the need to chase after love, acceptance, and fulfillment. He went to unimaginable lengths to chase the feeling of being valued, yet it only drove him to the darkest place in his life. He had spent all he had and came to the end of himself. Once his money was gone, his so-called friends and "fame" vanished as well. He was, alone, poor, and desperate.

So there he was at the lowest of all lows. Not only did he lose his personal wealth, but a famine swept the land and he began taking care of his pigs for work. I picture him thinking, "I've done everything I know to do, and look at me, I'm still unhappy. I tried so hard." Similar to when life throws us curveballs that leave us feeling overwhelmed and alone, the man in the story found himself on his hands and knees, more than ready to eat the scraps the pigs were eating. Everything he had tried in his own strength failed. Nothing could satisfy the emptiness. Seeking to win the acceptance of other people and living the "ideal" or "perfect life" did not fill the void in his soul. Striving in his own strength, he was not able to change a single thing.

I can only imagine the brokenness he must have been experiencing. Surely personal shame and regret consumed him. He had thrown away his time and his money, hurt his family, and disappointed himself. Yet in the midst of his loneliness, shame, and regret, the light bulb finally went on and he had a plan. He realized he could return home — not as a son; he had gone way too far for that — but as a servant. He was convinced his wrong actions made him unworthy to be counted a son, but he still had a sliver of hope that his works could pay for what he no longer deserved.

On his journey home, the son mentally prepared a little speech he would give his father when he saw him. "Because of everything I've done wrong, because of the way I used you, rejected and abandoned you, because of how I disappointed you (and myself), there is no way I could ever ask you to continue to love me. I went too far, and now it is too late to change the mistakes I have made. There is no way I can still be considered a son of yours. However if you will allow it, please let me work for you as a servant."

But think about this: Jesus said that while the son was still a long way off, compassion swept over the father the moment he saw his son. (That makes me think the father must have been watching for his son. The father never stopped thinking about him, hoping, "Maybe today will be the day that he comes back home.") The moment he saw his son, the father dropped everything he was doing and ran to him, wrapping his arms around him. I picture the son jumping back in utter shock, shouting, "Wait! You don't understand! I've done so much wrong. I'm not worthy to be called your son. I don't deserve your love."

We've now reached my favorite part of the story.

The father paid no attention to what his son said. He didn't take time to consider his son's prepared speech and think,

"Hmmm, wait a minute. He does make a good point. He really did put me through a lot of heartache. Maybe I should wait to see how he acts this time around. After all he has put me through, he needs to earn the right to be my son. He can't just prance back into our lives like nothing ever happened!"

No! Those thoughts never crossed the father's mind. He didn't think twice. Instead, he turned to his servants and said bring *quickly* the best robe, in fact, the festive robe of honor, and put it on him. Then he gave his son a ring for his finger and sandals for his feet. He also called for the biggest calf to be killed. He didn't care where his son had been, he was just happy to finally have him home! He said, "Let us revel and feast and be happy and make merry, because this my son was dead and is alive again. He was lost and is found" (Luke 15:23–24).

What a beautiful picture of the love that God has for you! He does not want you trapped under a load of condemnation and guilt. Your Father God does not want you stuck in chains of regret. He looks directly at you and says, "You are my child! I don't care where you have been, I want you! You belong to me!"

In the story, the son was convinced his value had been diminished by his actions and decisions. He was fully persuaded that because of what he had done, he was "no longer worthy" to be called a son.

How often do we feel no longer worthy? How many times do we rehash and replay our past failures and become consumed with our frustrations? We find ourselves accepting the lie that we are damaged goods, forever tainted by the things we have gone through. In our eyes, our worth begins to diminish as we begin to believe that our identity and our failures are one in the same. We automatically lose sight of who we are because we are blinded by what we have done in our past. We feel the need to pay for our past and work to make up for our sins. We assume

God must view us the same way we view ourselves, and we jump to the conclusion that He, too, cannot see beyond the things we have done.

When we allow our mistakes and disappointment to rob us of our self-value, it is easy to believe we are not good enough to be loved by God. When we do not love ourselves, we often question why a God who is perfect would ever love us. It is easy to get so focused on the past that we shrink back and feel we no longer deserve to be called His child. We put up an invisible wall of shame because we do not believe we are worthy to be close to Him.

This can cause us to run away from God as we search endlessly, trying to find something to give us temporary relief and fill that void in our hearts. Like the son in the story, we become obsessed with trying to attain the "next" thing on our list thinking, "Maybe if I can get him to like me, maybe if I live there," or "maybe if I get that job, I'll be happy." When that fails, we are still so desperate for happiness that we try to do enough good, becoming hard on ourselves, attempting to be perfect as we serve God merely as slaves, trying to please Him with our works.

Just for the record, God is not interested in your works apart from your relationship with Him as Father and child. He has no part in dead religion. Galatians 4:7 reassures you that, "You are no longer a slave (bond servant) but a son; and if a son, then [it follows that you are] an heir by the aid of God, through Christ." Let me make this clear: God is not looking for servants and slaves. Jesus died and was raised again so that you could be brought into the family as a beloved child! You are a child of the King, which means you are an heir. Unceasing love belongs to you. Confidence belongs to you. Freedom belongs to you. He is not a God of condemnation, and He takes no pleasure in any amount of guilt. That is not His character at all.

God does not require or desire that you work to pay for your past. In fact, He looks at your righteousness and striving to be "good enough" as filthy rags. He is the Father of all fathers and He loves you with everything He is. He simply wants you to receive and enjoy what He has freely given through Jesus.

Just like the father in the story, God does not want another day to pass by with you feeling like you are not good enough, seeing yourself as a failure. The son thought that his actions made him unworthy to be loved and that they had the power to change the way his father viewed him. He thought his father had forgotten about him. However, nothing was further from the truth. Not only had the father never stopped loving him, but he had continually dreamed of the day he would return. When he finally did return, the father didn't just put up with him. He was more than eager to celebrate him, simply because he was his son.

Father God feels the same way about you. In Jeremiah 31:3, He says to you, "I've never quit loving you and never will. Expect love, love, and more love" (MSG). Nothing you have or haven't done has the power to change that. His love is completely unstoppable! He will never quit loving you. You are God's favorite topic. He can't forget about you because He can't stop thinking about you! You are always on His mind and His love for you knows no end. He is saying, "You are mine and you have been made worthy of My love."

God does not just put up with you, He puts you up! He welcomes you into His open arms, puts you in the palm of His hand, and raises you up out of shame into newness of life. You are seated with Jesus in heavenly places, far above defeat, safe in His abounding grace. God puts a robe around your shoulders, honors you with His love, puts sandals on your feet, a ring on your finger and boldly declares, "You are My child! It's party time!" Revel in the Son's sacrifice, feast on that freedom, and bask in the victory that He won just for you!

Daddy's Little Girl

When I was going through my divorce, one of the things I dreaded the most actually turned into one of the most comforting, tangible expressions of love. For so long, I had made the mistake of bottling up all of the personal distress, emotional pain, and pressure I was dealing with. I have since learned that this hurts not only us, but also those closest to us.

Yet, feelings of torment and deep shame attached themselves to me. I was afraid of what other people would now think of me and wondered how things would ever be the same again. The thought of having to pick up the pieces of my life was overwhelming. So I allowed fear to keep me silent. But one thing I feared the most was how my own dad would respond when I finally told him that his little girl was getting a divorce. I tried for so long to look like I was happy and had a happy life because that's what I so desperately wanted. I was lugging around this huge burden, trying to hide the pain behind my smile, but nothing I tried could rid me of the disappointment I had in myself. I was constantly tormented, wondering if my dad's view of me would now match the disappointment and shame I had in myself.

When I couldn't take it any longer, I finally mustered up the courage to face my dad. I remember the exact moment, where we were sitting, and what we were doing. With a trembling voice, the facade I had created finally crumbled, and the truth of my pain was exposed.

Then the unimaginable took place right before my eyes. As I was sinking in my shame and guilt, like a fearless, conquering hero, my dad wrapped his loving arms around me, rested his head against mine, and gently whispered in my ear, "It's going to be okay." The compassion in his eyes and the love in his voice did more for me than I ever expected. That was all I needed to hear.

My dad did not judge me based on my situation. He did not beat me when I was already down. No! When I finally poured out my heart to him, his heart broke for mine. He didn't see me as damaged goods. He didn't view me as unclean. He didn't push me away, out of His sight. He didn't leave because He was so ashamed. No, not at all!

Not only did my dad not go away, he came closer. He got up from his chair and came to where I was, and drowned my grief with the most comforting, healing hug I have ever received. Waves of love and compassion radiated from his core and I realized how absurd and futile my previous fears had been. My transparency brought fresh freedom and light. With no barriers remaining, my dad cried with me, encouraged me, comforted me, and most importantly, he let me know we were going to get through it together.

I cannot begin to say how thankful and blessed I am to have such a strong man of love in my life.

Even though I am a grown woman, nothing still brightens my heart more than seeing how my relationship with my natural dad has continued to blossom and grow stronger. Honesty and communication are two matchless components and nothing can replace just being real with those you can trust. I am proud to be a "Daddy's Girl!" Yet, as wonderful as encouragement from people can be, nothing can take the place of the unconditional love, approval, and comfort of your Father God.

No Longer Slaves

You are never alone and your Father God knows everything you have been through. Because of His amazing love for us, God does not stop with simply saving us. When we believe in Jesus, God honors us and actually sends His very own Spirit to live on the inside of us.

Romans 8:15 says, "For [the Spirit which] you have now received [is] not a spirit of slavery to put you once more in bondage to fear, but you have received the Spirit of adoption [the Spirit producing sonship] in [the bliss of] which we cry, Abba (Father)! Father!" I love this scripture! As a child of the King, you have God's Holy Spirit living on the inside of you. God loves you so much that He desires to be with you ALWAYS.

Notice that the Holy Spirit is not a spirit of slavery. Having the mindset of the son in the story from Luke 15, desperately striving to be "good enough" to somehow make up for your past, is not living at all. Constantly being on edge to make sure you cross every "t" and dot every "i" is tormenting. That is a life of bondage and that is NOT the type of life that Jesus came to give you.

Jesus said, "I have come that they may have and enjoy life, and have it in abundance" (John 10:10). He not only wants you to have life, but to enjoy it! I guarantee that slaves do not live a free, joy-filled life. Jesus did not die and God did not raise Him up again just so you and I can go on living as slaves, tormented by the devil and intimidated by our past. You have not received the spirit of slavery to put you once more in bondage to fear, but you have the Spirit of adoption! This is Good News!

You do not have to go one more day living as a slave, in bondage trying to be good enough to earn the Father's love. You don't have to go another moment feeling subpar and beyond repair, unworthy of love and acceptance. Rid yourself of that false, slave identity. You are not a slave! You are not damaged goods! You are not defined by what lies behind! You are a child of the Most High King. God does not just tolerate you; *He celebrates you!* The Holy Spirit is the Spirit of love and He lets you know that you belong and you are wanted!

God's love takes away fear and expels every trace of torment. When the Source of love lets you know you are loved and that you belong, freedom springs forth. From that place of acceptance, we hear God boldly declare, "You are MY child! You belong! You are mine!" God is not ashamed of you. He is not disappointed in you. He claims you as His own. Yet, it does not end there.

Father of All Fathers

With hearts bubbling over with freedom, we can cry out, "Abba! Abba! Daddy God! I have a Father! I belong!" Shame has no place in His open arms. Regret is released when love sweeps in. Forgiveness and mercy radiate from the core of who He is and fear is dismissed. Just as a little child feels free to run up to the arms of her daddy, you can boldly run to your Father God at any time, any place, and in the middle of any situation.

It is vital to understand God never intended for you to go through the pain you've experienced. Please know that it was not His will for you to experience that abuse or rejection or whatever else you might have faced. One preacher said, "The reason bad things happen to good people is because people have a free will." John 10:10 reminds us, "The thief comes not but to kill, steal, and destroy." The devil is always looking for a way to steal from the life that Jesus came to give you, and he often uses other people or even our own wrong decisions to do his work.

If you have been abandoned by someone you thought you could trust — rejected by someone who was supposed to love you, experienced a tragic loss, or have been abused emotionally, verbally, sexually, or physically or if your personal failures have left you in a place of shame and desperation, first of all, with all that's in me, I am so sorry you went through that. God did not plan that for you. Nothing in Him wanted that to happen. It breaks your Father God's heart to see His precious child endure the struggles you have experienced and He understands the pain you have gone through.

Jeremiah 29:11 says, "For I know the thoughts and plans that I have for you, says the Lord, thoughts and plans for welfare and peace and not for evil, to give you hope in your final outcome." God only has good plans for your life. No matter where you are today, there is hope for you! God wants to take what the devil meant for bad and turn it around in your life, as you experience His healing love like never before. God is far greater than any pain. He has a plan of restoration for you. Because He loves you, God desires to heal your heart from every wound and make all things new.

And I am so sorry if you have had an unhealthy father figure or maybe no father figure at all. If the word "dad" carries with it some negative connotations, I want you to know that God is the Father like no other Father. He will NEVER walk out on you or give up on you. He is the Father you have always wanted, a Father beyond your greatest dreams.

I understand that society and negative experiences try to force us into the mold of empty arrogance. "I'm independent. I'm strong. I don't need anyone else." I understand how it's almost an automatic reflex to put up a shell to protect yourself after you experience hurt, rejection, or heartbreak. However, I also know that no matter what you have gone through, no matter what your age, within the heart of every individual is a longing for their Creator. The details of your story may be different from my story, but the answer is always the same. We all thirst for the love of the Father, which is only found through Jesus Christ. Regardless of how old we are or what we've experienced, we never stop wanting a Father who loves us unconditionally.

In the eyes of God, you are and will forever be His precious child. Let me tell you, there is nothing like having your Daddy

God wrap His arms of love around you. My experience continues to affirm that no matter our age and no matter what we go through, we always need a daddy, and God is the very best Daddy there ever will be! I promise He wants to be that to you. He is the only One who can fill that void in your heart. You may try to fill it with relationships, work, sex, or your number of social media followers. You may even attempt to divert your attention or deny that the void is there, desperately seeking value and crossing any and all lines to get the approval of others. But only God can heal a broken heart.

I understand the pain when people disappoint us or when we disappoint ourselves. Yet, it is time to rip off those Band-Aids we have used for so long to cover up the emptiness and disguise the brokenness. God no longer wants you to smile to try to hide your pain. No, He desires for you to have real joy that radiates from so deep within, you just can't help but smile!

When we finally come to the end of ourselves, letting go of our own efforts to fix ourselves, we can allow God to come in and flood our hearts with His grace. Our Father is the only One who can fill the void and take the broken pieces of our lives and turn them into something more beautiful than we could ever imagine! When God heals a broken heart, He doesn't just cover it up with a Band-Aid. He doesn't leave any scars. He leaves no residue of the past. He restores and makes new! He heals from the inside out and makes us whole. His presence floods us with a peace that passes all understanding, a peace that is greater than our past, a peace we cannot get anywhere else. We are assured that we are complete in Jesus and filled with a fresh hope! No more smiling to hide the pain; our smiles now come from a heart that has been healed and made whole. How beautiful it is to live each day knowing that you are loved and celebrated by One who has a plan of freedom and freshness for your life, One who not only wants to be God to you, but Who also wants to be the Father you have always dreamed of having!

I know that we cannot trust every single person People are not perfect, but your Father God is! God will never disappoint you. It is absolutely impossible for Him to fail you — He never has and He never will. Because He loves you with an unchanging love, you can trust Him without reservation. As the old saying goes, "Father knows best."

He knows how to completely transform that mess in your life by His grace and how you can live free from your past. All we have to do is to come to Him and trust Him to make all things new.

Life was not meant to be lived alone. Don't make the same mistakes I made. Don't allow the pressure to be perfect, the drive to be strong and independent, the fear of what people may think, or the hurts of your past keep you from opening up to people in your life. Ask God for the right friends and be brave to talk about what you are going through. You don't have to go through it alone. Above all else, remember that you can talk to your Father God about absolutely anything. He has wisdom for today and you will be strengthened by His presence. Your Father is so in love with you; you are the apple of His eye. God is not condemning you; you are valuable to Him. He knows everything we have done and everything we have been through. He wants you to know you are not alone. You are not forgotten. God cares about you individually and He is on your side. He is not a far-away God who is too busy for you. He is the Father who can't stop smiling when He thinks about you. You are constantly on His mind; He cares about you and watches over you tenderly.

If something matters to you, it matters to God. He is the Father who knows you by name, knows how many hairs are on your head, and gave everything He had just to get you back. The thoughts He thinks towards you are more in number than the grains of sand at the sea. God wants you to know you can trust Him. You can abandon yourself to Him. Cast all of your cares upon Him, because He cares for you (1 Peter 5:7). You can stop pretending, tear down the facade and run into His arms of love, peace, and fulfillment. He is not looking for perfect people. It's okay if things are not perfect; God will not give up on you. He will turn it around for your good if you will trust Him. In His freedom, you are made whole. He wants to comfort you like no one else can and cause you to move forward in the wonderful plan of restoration He has for you. There is no rejection in Jesus. There is no condemnation for anyone who is in Christ. Jesus has no part in shame and guilt. The blood of Jesus was shed for you individually. Jesus was and is perfect so the pressure is taken off of us to try to be. God does not expect nor require us to be perfect in our own strength. I know sometimes we look at ourselves and think, "I'm not good enough. I'm not tall enough, I'm not thin enough, or I can't do that good enough." But let me tell you this – you are enough in Jesus.

We no longer have to go on living as slaves, in bondage to trying to be good enough. God gave us the spirit of adoption! Because of Jesus and His blood that was poured out for us, we are now accepted and perfect in Him. His blood has taken away our past and cleansed us from our sins. We are made brand new in Jesus! He has given us a fresh start. We are enough! What Jesus did, He did for us. It was as if we did it.

You are not defined by what lies behind. You have been made brand new and complete in Christ. You have a new identity and an unchanging value in Jesus! He is so much greater than anything in your past. When God forgives, He chooses to forget. He is not like some people you may have encountered who say they forgive you but secretly hold on to your mistakes and then explode the moment you make the next one. God will never do that! He is not wishy-washy, He is not up and down, and He does not hold grudges. We never have to be afraid to come to Him.

The blood of Jesus does not just cover up our sins, but it reaches down and completely plucks that ugly thing out from its roots. His blood destroys it. Through His death, Jesus overcame the power of death. Sin has been deprived of its power. Death could not hold Jesus down and now, shame can't hold you down! When God raised Jesus from the dead, you were raised up with Him and have been seated in heavenly places, empowered by an abundance of grace and God's righteousness to rule and reign in this life. Jesus took you from the control of darkness, placed you in His kingdom of love, and set you free from sin, condemnation and guilt. You are now empowered to be more than a conqueror through Him who loves you!

The Holy Spirit takes no pleasure in seeing us wallow in the mistakes of our past, outside the palace doors because we feel unworthy to be loved. It's time to let go of that old slave mentality. This is not the end. You are a child of the Most High King! Condemnation is a thief and God has no part in it. He is not a god of condemnation; He is the God of restoration. He doesn't want you to waste another minute on guilt. Doubt does not please Him, faith does. Doubt causes us to question God's love and the power of the blood of Jesus to remove our sin. Doubt keeps us out. Yet, faith believes that this guilt-free life exists. Faith takes us into a whole new way of living. Faith opens up the door to the miraculous and allows us to live life the way God intended it to be lived. This pleases God because with all of His heart, He desires for us to live a free, satisfying, joy-filled life in Him. Have faith in His love for you and have faith in the precious blood that was shed for you. Believe and receive the Father's great love. Hear God boldly declare that it is party time, time to celebrate what Jesus, the perfect Lamb, did for you!

CHAPTER 4

FOREVER FAITHFUL

It is because of the Lord's mercy and loving-kindness that we are not consumed, because His [tender] compassions fail not. They are new every morning, great and abundant is your stability and faithfulness.

Lamentations 3:22–23

What glorious freedom and wonderful good news we get from these verses in Lamentations! God has endless mercy to match His endless love. Not only are His mercies new every morning, empowering you to walk out your fresh start without fear, but He is our stable and faithful Father. He changes not, so He can be depended on. Jesus Christ is the same yesterday, today, and forever.

Your actions will never cause your Father to love you any less or any more than He already does. God is love and He loves you individually with everything that He is. He is constant. He is constantly with you and for you, and you are constantly on His mind. He will never change His opinion of you; He will never think less of you or see you as "damaged goods" because of what you have done in the past. Great and abundant is His stability and faithfulness! He will never walk out on you, and He will faithfully complete what He has started in your life. Rest assured, God is not going anywhere, so His love is not going anywhere. He has got your back and He is working all things together for your good. Far too many have the wrong perception of God. Thousands believe that God is mad at them. Many have an image of God as someone who is always frustrated, always serious, and too busy with the important matters of the world to care about them. They may not admit it, but they have allowed the lie that God is greatly disappointed and hopelessly ashamed of them to take root. Yet, nothing could be further from the truth. I believe that one of the top things the devil is adamant about getting people to doubt is that God cares about them. Even the disciples had to deal with this.

Peace in the Storm

In Mark chapter 4, Jesus said to His disciples, "Let us go to the other side of the lake," so they loaded up into a boat and off they went, fully expecting to make it to their destination. However, something happened in the middle of their journey. A huge storm came out of nowhere. The winds were raging and the waves beat against the sides of the boat. Fear gripped the disciples and they were frantic for their lives.

As quickly as the water began to flood the boat, I am certain that questions flooded the minds of the disciples: "Why is this happening to us? We are good people. We are doing something good! We are even helping Jesus! Why would Jesus let this happen to us!? Why did He tell us to go to the other side if this storm was coming? Where is Jesus?" Overwhelmed, afraid, and confused, they finally found Jesus *asleep in the back of the boat!* With great frustration they cried out, "Do You not care that we are perishing?"

Wow. Out of everything they could have possibly said, that was the one question in the forefront of their minds. That one question jumped out of their mouths, revealing their doubts. Because of the storm they encountered, they did not believe that Jesus truly cared about them.

The devil is persistent in using situations — what other people have done to us, said to us, and even our own failures — to make us feel hopeless, alone, and unwanted. He will point at circumstances and whisper in our ears, "If God really loved you, why did He let that happen?" The devil is heartless and He will use the most tragic of situations, the very moments you most need to rely upon the love and grace of your Father, to set you against God by convincing you He is against you. The devil is a liar and a thief, and he will lie to you about God, trying to steal a life of peace from you.

Always remember, God is the giver of life and all good things. God is good. The devil is bad. As simple as that is, we must never get the two mixed up. God never works alongside the devil to try to teach us a lesson. God never has and never will take away babies because "He needed another angel in the choir." God will never put sickness and disease on us to try to "teach us to trust because He knows what we need more than we do." No! Those are all lies straight from the pit of hell.

The devil's one aim is to kill, steal, and destroy. He is on a mission to use whatever he can to get you to run away from God and not trust Him. He will look for any way possible to steal your life and joy, destroy your opinion of yourself, deprive you of confidence, and break your heart. However, he won't stop there. When he causes horrific things, he will put the blame on God.

How many times have you heard people say, "If God is really such a good God, then why are there so many orphans starving in the world? Why are there so many tragedies? Why are there so many storms that kill people? Why did this happen to me?" The devil is an expert blame-shifter.

Let's go back to the disciples on the boat with Jesus. Because of the storm they faced, fear gripped their hearts and they doubted if Jesus cared about them. Yet what did Jesus do? With great boldness and love, Jesus got up and spoke to the winds and the sea. He rebuked them and said, "Peace, be still." Instantly, there was a great calm. Then Jesus turned to His disciples with a question for them. Jesus asked, "Why are you so fearful and intimidated? Where is your faith?"

And think about this. If Jesus was the author of that tragic storm, why would He rebuke it and command it to leave? And why would Jesus stay in the boat with the disciples? You see, Jesus was able to be at complete peace even smack dab in the middle of the most tragic situations because His heart was anchored in the unfailing love of His Father. He had faith in God's limitless love for Him.

Jesus lived on this earth as a man just like us. In doing so, He showed us the type of life we are free to live — a life of authority and boldness, marked by a fearlessness that comes from knowing that your Father loves you unconditionally. Because He knew how much His Father loves Him, He was at peace while others panicked. First John 4:18 says that perfect love casts fear out and expels every trace of terror. When you know how much God loves you, you know that He is right there with you. He's got your back, and you can rise up with boldness in the middle of any situation, command peace to reign and speak out what God says about you. No matter what waves try to shake you, you can have peace in the midst of the storm since you know that God will turn the situation around for your good, all because He loves you. Like Jesus spoke to the winds and the waves, speak to any shame and inferiority and command it to leave your life. You are loved and you have authority.

The enemy knows that if we doubt God's love, we are doubting who He is. Without the stability that comes from having God's love as the foundation of who we are, our lives would be a roller coaster of emotions and we would be doomed to a fearful, hopeless existence. The Father's love is what gives meaning to our lives. Jesus gives us our unchanging value and He defines who we are. The disciples grew frantic and lost hope so Jesus asked them, "Where is your faith?" When we choose to believe the love that God has for us and we deposit all of our faith in that love, we can live with the same stability and fearlessness as Jesus.

We can rest in God's perfect love because He is faithful to work all things together for our good and He will take us to the finish line. We are gonna make it! No matter where life may find us, we can live with our souls anchored upon the Solid Rock because His mercies are new every morning and GREAT is His stability! The winds and the waves may try to knock us down but they cannot conquer us as long as we do not quit. We can live stable, peaceful lives in every season of life. God is faithful. God is stable. God is love. We do not ever have to cross our fingers that He is in a good mood. We never have to wonder if He is still there and if He still cares about us. We never have to be afraid to come to Him, to run boldly to His throne. He is the God of great mercy and compassion. We can cast all of our cares upon Him because He cares about us watchfully and tenderly.

Even in the midst of storms, we never have to ask Jesus if He cares about us, as the disciples did, because God already gave us the answer, and His answer is still the same today: "Yes, I have loved you with an everlasting love; therefore with loving-kindness have I drawn you and continued My faithfulness to you" (Jeremiah 31:3).

No matter what storms of life you may be facing, remember what Jesus said, "Let us go to the other side!" because God is faithful.

No Greater Desire

The statement, "Where there's a will, there's a way" reminds me of an experience in an airport while flying back to Miami from Paris, running on about two hours of sleep. Flight delay after delay continued to push my limits and found me dozing off on foreign airport floors. When I finally arrived on U.S. soil in a New York airport, I was informed once again that I was going to be delayed, which would not only cause me to go more hours without sleep, but also completely ruin some much-anticipated plans I had made for my arrival in Miami.

Before I continue, let me explain that me not getting enough sleep is a bad idea — a *very* bad idea. To this day, I still get teased about how cranky I can be when I'm tired. With that being said, maybe you won't judge me quite as much when I tell you what happened next. Well, to put it lightly, something on the inside of me snapped. Let me just say that right there and then, I lost my usually polite demeanor, and I began to make a horrendous scene at the ticket counter.

The moment I saw the look of embarrassment on my sister's face, I knew I had to get it together. And I also knew that the only thing that could possibly get me somewhat back to normal would be some frozen yogurt in my stomach as soon as possible, preferably before I hurt somebody.

If you are anything like me, you'll agree that frozen yogurt is much more than just a good idea and is certainly suitable for breakfast, lunch, or dinner — or all three meals all day, every day. We all know there are magic powers hidden in the swirly goodness of those brightly colored soft-serve machines. God is helping me with my sugar addiction, but I am a firm believer that while only God can heal a broken heart, only "froyo" can calm the nerves and bring immense joy. Well, maybe that's not entirely true, but it definitely helps!

So the hunt was on. I had no idea if there was a froyo machine within the JFK airport, but I knew I was going to search until I found one and even take a taxi into the city if I needed to. My game face was on and power walking was in full force. I had a strong desire for something, and I was going to do whatever it took to get it.

Finally the search was over, and I kissed the counter of the glorious frozen yogurt establishment. From the very first bite, my hormones slowly began to balance and each gram of sugar brought life back to my soul. However, one serving was not going to be enough. As I was leaving the line, I heard a customer say that her order was messed up and she handed her chocolate yogurt back to the cashier. Before the cashier had a chance to throw the cone away, without thinking I grabbed it out of the server's hands and like a crazy woman blurted out, "I'll take it." Finally at a place of peace and contentment, I walked away with not one, but two servings of yummy, calming goodness. My desire was satisfied.

I'm sure you know that when you have a strong enough longing for something, you will do whatever it takes to satisfy that desire. Let me reassure you that there is *no greater desire* in the universe than the longing within your Father's heart to lavish His love on you. He yearns to have you experience the freedom of His love every single day of your life.

But God—so rich is He in His mercy! Because of and in order to satisfy the great and wonderful and intense love with which He loved us, 5 Even when we were dead (slain) by [our

own] shortcomings and trespasses, He made us alive together in fellowship and in union with Christ.

Ephesians 2:4–5

Your Father God is never going to stop loving you and He is never going to stop calling you by name. He will never stop saying, "You are Mine!" His mercy is just too great. That mercy never runs out or expires and it is greater than anything you have ever done or been because He is greater than all. God loves prostitutes, lesbians, drug addicts, teen moms, preachers who screw up, and religious people who are bound to their perfectionism. God loves you unconditionally. He has a plan of freedom. You are forever safe in the palm of His hand, free from rejection and condemnation. He is constantly giving more mercy when you least deserve it, when you mess up in the same area thousands of times, when you knew better, no matter what, He will never stop flooding you with His mercy.

Just like one bowl of froyo is not enough, the love of God is so great, so wonderful, so intense, that He is compelled to pour out an extravagant dosage of mercy upon you. Where there is a will, there is a way and trust me, there is no stronger will than that of God who wants you to know His love and let it transform your life. He will do whatever it takes to get His love to you. I knew that if there was a single froyo machine in the entire JFK airport, I would find it. God knows the way to your heart. His eyes are constantly scanning the earth, searching for a way to show you His goodness and demonstrate His love to you. Trust me, He will do whatever it takes to find the way to let you know how much you mean to him.

You are on God's mind at every moment of every day. That is why when you wake up in the morning, He says, "You are Mine. I love you. Here are new mercies for you today." When you mess up 15 minutes later, He does not change. He says, "You are Mine, I believe in you. Here is some more mercy." Even in the middle of beating yourself down, cutting yourself, as you are taking those drugs, if you will just listen, you can hear Him say, "My child, you don't have to do that. You are so precious to Me. Here is some more mercy, for no other reason than because I love you. Remember, I have set you free." In the middle of the night, He whispers, "I'm right here, I'm not going to leave you. Dream of My mercy tonight. Dream of how I am going to bless you all the days of your life."

According to Ephesians 2:7, there is nothing that God desires more than to "clearly demonstrate through the ages to come the immeasurable (limitless and surpassing) riches of His free grace in His kindness and goodness of heart toward us in Christ Jesus." God will go beyond the limits, do the unimaginable, whatever it takes to satisfy His intense desire to show you how much He loves you. He will not quit until His craving to bless you is satisfied. He knows the thoughts and plans that He has for you, plans to give you hope in your final outcome. That sounds like a beautiful plan of never-ending, mercy to me! You are His masterpiece and He has the good life ready and waiting for you to live it!

The Rest You've Been Looking For

Come to Me, all you who labor and are heavy-laden and overburdened, and I will cause you to rest. [I will ease and relieve and refresh your souls.] Take My yoke upon you and learn of Me, for I am gentle (meek) and humble (lowly) in heart, and you will find rest (relief and ease and refreshment and recreation and blessed quiet) for your souls. For My yoke is wholesome (useful, good—not harsh, hard, sharp, or pressing, but comfortable, gracious, and pleasant), and My burden is light and easy to be borne.

Matthew 11:28

Jesus will relieve, and refresh your discouraged soul. He has more than enough refreshment for you! However, before that can fully take place, we must do what Jesus said and take His yoke upon ourselves and learn of Him.

In farming, a yoke is used as a harness to join oxen together, connect them to a plow, and guide them as they work the fields. The devil wants to put his yoke upon you and keep you in bondage, forcing you to lug around depression and shame. He wants to make your life hard and pressing so you feel the need to work for approval and forgiveness. By keeping you stuck in guilt, the enemy desires to control the direction of your life while he wreaks his havoc on your soul.

His purpose in all this is so you question your worth and purpose. By influencing you to draw your sense of value from the opinions of others, your performance, your relationship status, your body weight, or anything else that has the ability to change. Satan wants you to focus on your imperfections. Believe me, in his persistent attempt to destroy your life, he will try anything and everything to get you to question the fact that you are unconditionally loved.

Yet in the midst of carrying the devil's yoke, Jesus has the freedom your soul has been longing for! With relentless love, Jesus says, "Come to Me!" And when you do, you find peace for your soul.

A life of shame and regret is an exhausting life. Living under a load of intimidation and stress, working to win the approval of others, is not truly living. It is mentally and physically draining to try to earn something we could never deserve in our own striving.

That is why Jesus says, "Come to Me! ALL who labor and are overburdened" (Matthew 11:28). No one is excluded from His free invitation to experience His great grace. You are not a lost cause and you have not gone too far. Your Father does not want you to spend one more moment under the heavy burden of condemnation. God is not sitting in heaven just waiting for you to mess up so He can beat you down even more. He is not a dictator; He is the God of great mercy. Jesus' yoke is not hard, sharp, or pressing and His burden is light. If He is not hard on you, you do not have to be hard on yourself. If God has forgiven you, you can forgive yourself. Remember, a negative opinion of yourself does not change how God sees you. His opinion is the right one. Let the way He sees you change the way you see yourself. You are loved and you are forgiven.

The Bible says the devil roams around like a lion, looking for the slightest opening to creep in and devour our lives (1 Peter 5:8). He tries to load us down with burdens. He wants to put the weight of sin and guilt upon our shoulders. He wants to see us crumble under the fear of others' opinions and the torment of our past. The enemy hopes that we get stuck right where we are at so the years pass us by as we remain bound by chains of regret, past hurts, and disappointments. He hopes that we'll run ourselves ragged, deceived into thinking that maybe dead works and religion will help us earn God's approval but never really convinced that we are ever good enough, no matter how hard we try.

Come to Jesus! His arms are wide open and His grace is more than enough for you! He will ease your burden and refresh your soul. The devil works tirelessly to weigh you down with his burdens and deception, but Jesus is the glory and the lifter of your head. There is no burden He cannot remove! All fears vanish in His perfect love. Remember, nothing can separate you from God's love. The only defense the devil has against God's love is deception. He will try so hard to deceive you into thinking your past has distanced you from God and has taken away His love, but all the while, God is right there gently whispering,

"I've never left you. I am right here and My love for you hasn't gone anywhere."

Quit trying to work for something that has already been freely given — just receive the gift of God's approval! You can try to run away, but His love will never fade. It is relentless and His goodness is the very thing that draws you to Him. Quit trying to fix yourself and live in your strength. Simply come to Jesus. Intimidation and feelings of inferiority are deprived of their power in the light of who He is. His grace covers you and destroys every weight. You need not spend one more moment with your head hung in shame; you have been set free by the love of Jesus to live with your shoulders back and your head lifted high!

When we are under the burden of shame with our heads hung low, every reason why we are unworthy is before our eyes, eating away at our soul. We are consumed with thoughts of what others have done to us and all the reasons we do not measure up. However, Jesus is the lifter of our head and He is giving us a fresh start with a new perspective. If the Son has set us free, we are free indeed!

Death could not hold Jesus down and you have been raised to share in that new life with Him. That means that guilt and condemnation have been rendered powerless. Shame does not have to hold you down one more day. You do not have to let any dark residue of the past fester in your soul. Jesus removes the burden and His words bring light and freedom. You are seated with Him in heavenly places. From this new perspective, you are able to gaze upon the beauty of His great love for you. See it! Open up your eyes! Behold and marvel at the sight of this matchless love that has been poured out on you!

Since before you were born, your Father God has been mindful of your name and He picked you out for Himself. He chose you then, and you are His first choice today. Nothing has ever changed that. Today, right where you are at, He is still calling your name. Jesus' arms were hung wide open on the cross and He continues to keep His arms of love wide open, inviting you to come to Him. Don't try to clean yourself up first, don't think about what you can try to do to become "better." Abandon all of that and run fearlessly to your Father. In this very moment, all God sees is you — beautiful you — his masterpiece. All He wants you to see is Jesus, all that He did for you, and His unending love for you. You are not a mistake. This world would not be better off without you. You are irreplaceable and you are God's very own.

Jesus said in John 14:27, "Peace I leave with you; My [own] peace I now give and bequeath to you. Not as the world gives do I give to you. Do not let your hearts be troubled, neither let them be afraid. [Stop allowing yourselves to be agitated and disturbed; and do not permit yourselves to be fearful and intimidated and cowardly and unsettled.]" You do not have to live another day intimidated by your past or afraid of the future! Throw off the chains of regret and the bondage and come to Jesus! Do not let your heart be troubled, God is greater than your past. Take His yoke upon you, let Him direct your life and then receive the relief that He has for your soul. He wants to restore your life and strengthen you in every way. Jesus is offering a permanent vacation of rest for your soul.

The peace of Jesus is far greater than any trial. His peace surpasses all understanding, which means you can stay calm, cool, and collected when it doesn't even make sense! You could be wondering, "Wait, all this is wrong right now, they are doing all of this against me, how do I still have peace?" Just come to Jesus. Trust Him. Keep your mind stayed on Him and He will keep you in that place of perfect and constant peace. Worry may try to come, but your heart can remain unshaken as you declare, "My

God has got my back and He is working all things together for my good!"

Have you ever noticed that you become like those with whom you spend the most time? I tease my mom because without a doubt, every time we visit family in Tennessee, within five hours of being back in the mountains, my mom starts speaking with a country accent, saying "y'all" every other sentence! It is so easy to begin to think, talk, and act like those with whom we spend a lot of time. But that also means that as you spend more time with Jesus, you will begin to think the way He does, talk the way He does, and act the way He does. What better person is there to imitate? There is fullness of joy in His presence. He thinks good, happy thoughts about you! Let His attitude rub off on you. He will empower you to love yourself the way that He does. You can be happy with yourself because He certainly is. Because His yoke is easy and His burden is light, we need no longer beat ourselves down. God is not mad at you.

A New Name

You'll get a brand-new name

straight from the mouth of GOD.

You'll be a stunning crown in the palm of GOD's hand,

a jeweled gold cup held high in the hand of your God.

No more will anyone call you Rejected,

and your country will no more be called Ruined.

You'll be called Hephzibah (My Delight),

and your land Beulah (Married),

Because GOD delights in you

and your land will be like a wedding celebration.

For as a young man marries his virgin bride,

so your builder marries you,

And as a bridegroom is happy in his bride,

so your God is happy with you.

Isaiah 62:1–5, MSG

Did you get that!? God is a happy God and He is happy with you! What a beautiful passage of Scripture. God says he sets you on high like a jeweled cup. He's placed you in the palm of His hand and He lifts you up for all to see. Without any trace of hesitation, God gave everything He had just to get you. You forever have a place in the heart of your Father. He wanted you before you were born and He wants you now. He can't stop thinking about you and He never will. He cannot get you out of His heart — he doesn't He want to — because nothing brings Him greater joy than when He thinks about you.

No greater love was ever demonstrated than when Jesus freely laid down His life just for you. He went into the heart of the earth, destroyed the one who had the power of death, and has now taken you out of the control of darkness. What a conquering hero! He truly is the Champion of our souls.

Take that out and insert:

Jesus has given you freedom from your past so you can enjoy freedom in the present and walk into a future bursting with hope and new life. Live each day with God's love at the forefront of your thoughts. Remember that you were His idea and He chose you on purpose! There is absolutely nothing that you could ever do that could make God love you any more than He already does and there is nothing that you could do that could cause Him to love you any less. He is the Father of all fathers and He calls you His very own.

When Jesus was being baptized in the River Jordan, a voice from heaven said, "This is My Son, My Beloved, in Whom I delight" (Matthew 3:17). In my mind, I picture the clouds splitting and the sun acting as the ultimate spotlight, singling Jesus out of the crowd, as God's declaration of love for His Son was heard by all.

Because of everything that Jesus has done for us, we are safe and secure in Him. There is no rejection and no condemnation in Jesus! When we are found in our Savior, our identity is secure in Him. God loves us the exact same way that He loves Jesus — unconditionally and boldly. He is love and He loves to demonstrate His love! He is a God of action, showing us the proof of His boundless love. What He thinks about Jesus, He thinks about us. What He said to Jesus, He says to us.

The spotlight of His unfailing love is upon you right now! He has singled you out of the crowd, called you by name, and chosen you as His very own. Without any hesitation and without the slightest trace of shame in His voice, the Father is looking directly at you and boldly declaring your new name for all to hear, "THIS IS MY CHILD! This is the one I love! You are the child I dreamed of before the beginning of time. YOU WILL NOT BE REMEMBERED FOR THAT! No! You are the joy of my heart and the delight of my life! You are constantly in my thoughts and I have a future full of hope for you!"

Your Father God is happy with you and He smiles when He thinks about you. God is not the least bit disappointed in you and He will certainly not disappoint you! You can trust Him without any reservation. Right now, choose to believe the great love that He has for you. No longer live satisfied with just knowing about His love; decide to dive in and experience this living love for yourself. You belong and you are wanted. His love defines who you are and gives fresh meaning to your life. You are not the mistakes of your past; you are not your failures. You are celebrated and loved unconditionally. See the love in His eyes and hear the smile in His voice as He looks at you and says, "You will not be remembered for that. That is not who you are. You are My child. You belong. YOU ARE LOVED."

PART TWO

Loving Yourself

CHAPTER 5

THE STORY YOU BELIEVE ABOUT YOURSELF

In the same way that it is one thing to hear that Jesus loves you, but an entirely different matter to make the decision to bank your life on that living love; it is one thing to know God wholeheartedly adores you, but another to take that love one step further and love your own self as God loves you. Yes, that's right. God wants you to love *you*. What good is it to know that God delights in you if you continue to allow shame, frustration, and disappointment to fester in your soul and consume who you are? Even though God is always on your side and He is for you, if you are against yourself, you will live an empty, defeated life of regret.

I've heard it said that our lives are the result of the story we believe about ourselves. Accepting an unhealthy, false self-image stops a person in life. Every opportunity to succeed and every ingredient necessary for a fulfilling life could knock on the door of an insecure person, but if the individual does not believe he is enough, he will never answer it. He will continue on his walk of life, empty handed and discouraged. Life is never what it could be for those who are unhappy with themselves. On the other hand, even in the absolute worst of circumstances, a person who expects the best will always come out shining. It's not what you go through, it's what you choose to believe that makes the difference.

Your life will never go beyond the perimeters set by your own beliefs. You determine what is possible or impossible by what you believe. You decide what you can or can't do, who you are or who you're not, what you can be or what you'll never become. The choice is completely up to you. You set the limitations on your own life.

This truth reminds me of one of my favorite childhood stories, Watty Piper's classic, *The Little Engine that Could*. It's a story about a train that breaks down on its way to deliver toys to boys and girls on the other side of the mountain. In the train's moment of desperation, a little blue engine happens to go by. At first, the little engine is convinced he is too small to help because he has never pulled a train or even made it over the mountain before. However, the little engine, seeing the hopelessness of the train and the toys, decides to change what he believes about himself.

Puff by puff, the little engine starts pulling the heavy train while saying, "I think I can. I think I can. I think I can." Slowly, the little engine climbs higher and higher, all the while saying, "I think I can. I think I can." Up, up, up they go, until exuberant cheers break loose, announcing their victory. They made it over the mountain! With a bright smile, the little engine happily puffs away, chanting, "I thought I could. I thought I could. I thought I could."

By changing his thoughts, the little engine changed his reality. He stopped assuming it was impossible, and it became possible.

Can you think of a time when you talked yourself out of doing something you wanted to do? Have you ever convinced yourself that you couldn't do what you dreamed about or secretly thought you weren't good enough to have something you wanted?

Our past does not have to shape our future. We can live our lives based on the good we choose to believe about ourselves. Our expectations carry an undeniable magnetic force and our thoughts create our reality. Proverbs 23:7 (ISV) says, "For as he thinks within himself, so he is." The Good News Translation of Proverbs 4:23 says, "Be careful how you think; your life is shaped by your thoughts." In other words, what we think about, we actually bring about.

According to Romans 12, we are transformed by the renewing of our minds. Renewing our minds involves taking off the old and putting on the new. As we choose to think God's thoughts, letting go of what our past says about us, what others have done, and the lies we have accepted, our lives will change. Mark 9:23 (NKJV) declares, "*All* things are possible to him who believes." God's Word Translation puts it this way: "As far as possibilities go, everything is possible for the person who believes." And the Message Bible puts it this way, "There are no 'ifs' among believers. Anything can happen."

Wow! Did you get that? *Anything can happen*! I can't even begin to tell you how thrilled my heart was when I read that for the first time. I jumped around my house and danced with joy as I realized that a simple shift in our thinking is the very thing that can catapult us into an entirely new way of living.

If negative thinking confines our lives, we must let positive believing unleash the realm of possibilities! Renew your mind and see yourself the way God does. Believe and receive the love that He has for you and then love yourself the same way. He will restore your relationship with yourself. Believing will bring about the fulfillment of those wondrous things God has planned. Believe what He says about your future, that nothing will be impossible. Faithful is He who has called you and HE is faithful to do it. Your Father will complete what He has started, and He will never fail you!

The believing life is the happy life! What we choose to believe about ourselves determines the direction and quality of our lives. Believing what God has said about us and about our future is like joining forces with Him; it opens up the door for Him to do the miraculous. We do the believing and God does the impossible! We do the believing and He does the changing!

He has the power to change the way we view ourselves and He wants us to enjoy being the wonderful, unique person He has made us to be. God believes in you, now it's time to believe in yourself. Change the story you believe about yourself and watch God transform your life. Today, you can be set free to love yourself and be happy simply being you.

I love what Luke 1:45 says: "And blessed (happy, to be envied) is she who believed that there would be a fulfillment of the things that were spoken to her from the Lord." The King James version puts it this way, "And blessed is she that believed: for there shall be a performance of those things which were told her from the Lord."

What I Believed

When I was in the third grade, I remember comparing my average-sized thighs to the thighs of some very thin girls in my class whom I considered to be "popular." Because my thighs did not measure up, I believed I was not as pretty as the other girls.

As a result, I did not expect to be popular and guess what, I wasn't. In high school, I believed I was shy, therefore I acted shy. As a young adult, I rarely believed I was adequate compared to others, so I often remained in the shadows.

As the years went by, I found myself caught in a vicious comparison trap, believing that I was never enough. My self-worth slowly began to diminish. I did not see much value or beauty in myself apart from my "good performance." I became a people-pleaser, eager to gain my sense of value from the approval of others. I threw my own care to the side and made unhealthy decisions.

In my search for self-worth and fulfillment, I became a perfectionist. I was constantly hard on myself and when I messed up, I didn't know how to forgive myself. I felt like a complete failure, as I could not see a distinction between who I was and the mistakes I had made.

Overwhelmed and tormented in my soul, I started to physically abuse myself. This only escalated during the time of my divorce. I did not understand how to deal with my pain, frustration, and self-disappointment I had kept bottled up for so long. I was at a dark place in my life, dealing with things I never imagined I would face. I seriously considered taking my own life. At that moment in time, I didn't know how I could go on living with myself and the mistakes I had made. The vision and passion I once had for life was sucked out of me. I was bleeding on the inside, yet trying to hide my pain behind a smile.

Mirror, Mirror on the Wall

There were many decorative mirrors on the walls of my house. Because I had such a negative opinion of myself, I walked around with my head hung low. I could not stand to look at myself. I thought I was ugly in every way. I was convinced the things I had done made me a worthless, terrible person. I remember a specific time when seeing my reflection stirred up such self-hate, I punched the mirror, nearly shattering it.

Now that I think about it, my reflection in a broken mirror would have been an accurate representation of the shattered self-perception and brokenness that tormented my soul. I could not believe who I had let myself become. How had my life spiraled into hopelessness? Where was the happy girl I once had been?

Perhaps you are able to relate to my feelings of shame and self-disappointment. Maybe you have never felt as though you are enough. Can I just be real with you? For so long, I live dissatisfied with who I was. Rarely could I be around other people without comparing my personality to theirs. Those thoughts of comparison became more extreme thoughts of regret and self-hate; God had to teach me to love myself. To be perfectly honest, this is something I am still constantly learning. I don't believe that learning to love and accept ourselves is something we fully master within a week. I don't believe there is a five-step program that can make us suddenly say, "Wow, I'm glad I finally whipped that and I will never have to deal with comparison again!" Rather, it is a process we can always be growing in. Daily, we must choose to be thankful for who God has made us to be.

There are so many changes we will encounter throughout the course of our lives. We will go through relationship changes, age progressions, career shifts, body weight fluctuations, and many more things. In it all, we will have to live with the consequences of our choices and learn to be at peace with ourselves, even when we make mistakes, fail, or encounter difficult times. Through our failures and successes, our griefs and joys, we must remember to be patient with ourselves and enjoy the journey.

If we are ever going to live a happy life, we must first become happy with ourselves. If we are ever going to live a life that we love, we must first of all love ourselves. The choice is up to us whether or not we will truly live during that time and let that person we are on the inside, out.

First Corinthians 13:7 says, "Love bears up under anything and everything that comes, is ever ready to believe the best of every person, its hopes are fadeless under all circumstances, and it endures everything [without weakening]." This is God's description of what love looks like. Not only are we to love other people like this, but this is how we are to love ourselves because this is how God loves us. When you love yourself the way your Father God does, you will choose to believe the best about yourself.

No matter what others have done to you or what you have faced in the past, love endures without weakening or fading and it continues to believe what God says, regardless of contrary opinions and feelings. Go ahead, give yourself a second chance because God always does!

God knows that our quality of life is greatly dependent upon the type of relationship we have with ourselves. That may sound strange, but God loves us and He wants us to love ourselves so we can enjoy our lives. We are with ourselves more than we are with any other person. Think about it. When you wake up in the morning, you are right there. When you brush your teeth, you are there. When you go to work, you are always there. You may try to get away from it all and escape on vacation, but, boom! Guess who will be right there? There is no escaping yourself. That means that if we are going to enjoy our lives, we better learn how to be happy with ourselves.

Our actions will always reflect what we believe about ourselves. Like R.S. Grey said, "She believed she could, so she did." I like to say it this way, "She thought she was, so she is." I have finally realized that I am the one who decides if I am beautiful or not. I decide if I'm confident or not. I decide if I'm happy with myself or not. I decide what I can or cannot do.

When you believe you are beautiful, you will live radiantly. When you expect to have favor and expect people to like you, you light up the room with love. When you believe that you add value to the lives of others, you live fearlessly. When you believe that you are loved and that Jesus makes all things new, you live free. You have the power to decide what you will be remembered for.

Looking at the Front Side

I've heard the life of someone touched by God's grace described like a beautiful tapestry. From the back side, it looks like a tangled mess. The direction of the threads is confusing, the knots and frayed edges look frazzled and worthless. If we focus on the back, we see no beauty.

However, the front of the tapestry tells a whole other story. The finished product leaves us awestruck at its beauty and perfection. While looking at the back, we may be tempted to say, "Wait! Get rid of this big, ugly knot! What about this huge mess of tangled threads?" Yet, removing a single thread, no matter how messy and frayed it may appear, would alter the incredibly beautiful picture on the front.

This is the grace of Jesus! He loves you too much to leave you in your tangled mess of mental torment and pain. You do not have to stay stuck in regret and shame, wishing you never went through that experience or made those decisions. Your life will not be summed up by that regret and you will not be swallowed by shame. No, God's grace *is greater* than that! He has the power to remove all shame!

That means you and I do not have to waste any more days trapped in depression, crying about what we cannot change. We do not have to watch the years pass us by as we hopelessly relive our past. Let's quit wishing that thing never happened to us, quit crying about the time that we feel like we lost, and get up and do something about all of the time that we have left. Rise up in faith and look at what God is wanting to do RIGHT NOW. Regret keeps you stuck, but faith catapults you forward. We can't change what is behind us, but God can rearrange it all for your good. If you trust Him, He will turn every negative into a positive because He is so much greater than the storms of life.

The moment you catch a glimpse of where you are headed and how God is miraculously transforming that pain into your gain, you won't want to change a thing. Forget regret — it will get you nowhere and it will not fix a single thing. It will simply keep you paralyzed. Why waste time with regret when your future is so much greater? God has made a commitment to love you and He is saying, "Shake off the dust from the past! Let Me show you a glimpse of what is ahead, of how I'm turning this out for your good. Let your heart come alive within the beauty of what I have for you."

Rest assured, our Jesus is the Author and the Finisher! What He has started in your life, He will be faithful to complete. And guess what? He does not write any bad endings! Our Father is a strong believer in happy endings. That means that no matter what you might be facing, no matter how bad it may look right now, you can be strong and be encouraged. You are going to make it!

CHAPTER 6

WHAT JESUS THINKS

One day while Jesus was preaching, the scribes and Pharisees dragged in a woman who had been caught in the act of adultery and made her stand in the middle of the crowd as they accused her. Just imagine how humiliating that must have been for her. There she was, probably half-clothed, her shame exposed for all to see. In the eyes of her accusers, she didn't have an ounce of worth or even a name; they didn't even believe she had a right to continue living. She was defined by her failures.

The religious leaders measured her value according to the law, which commanded that "such women" must be stoned to death. "Such women" — that was the label that was given to her by the world. According to her past, they labeled her as damaged goods and placed her in a lower class where she would be kept in bondage by regret and feelings of inferiority. Each one of her accusers had a stone in hand, more than ready to ensure that the memory of her life would be summed up in one word — shame.

But as she stood in the midst of accusers eager to stone her, Jesus paused, stooped down, and began writing on the ground with His finger. Finally, He said to all those around, "Let him who is without sin among you be the first to throw a stone at her" (John 8:7).

The crowd was awestruck. Not a single soul expected such an answer. One by one they all left the scene, until Jesus was left alone with the woman. With tenderness and compassion, Jesus told her, "I do not condemn you either. Go on your way and from now on sin no more" (John 8:11).

One moment with Jesus forever changed everything in this precious woman's life. She came into His presence ashamed, accused, and condemned. She came burdened under the label of "damaged goods." Then Jesus changed everything. All because of what He did for her, she is not remembered as the adulterous woman, but she is remembered as the woman to whom Jesus gave a second chance. He did not condemn her and give her life up to destruction. Rather, He loved her and gave her a fresh start. Her accusers said, "Enough is enough, look at what she has done! This woman is worthless! She does not even deserve a name, much less the right to go on living." Religion looked at her past to determine her future. Yet Jesus' actions said, "I love you. When I look at you, I do not just see what you have done — I see you and I care about you. You are *not* damaged goods. You are *not* what you have done. You are *not* your failures. You are *not* what other people have said about you. You will not remain a captive of your past and your life will not be swallowed up by this shame. Your life will not be defined by what lies behind." To them, she was nameless, but to Him, she was shameless and priceless.

Right now, with His eyes full of compassion, Jesus is looking directly at you and saying the same thing. He is saying, "When I see you, I see value, I see beauty, I see worth. You were worth giving My life for. You are worth a second chance. Your life is not over. I am with you and I am going to take this exact moment and turn it around for your good. What was intended to consume you with shame, I'm going to transform as a catalyst for you to go further than you ever imagined. I will cause this very moment to be the fresh start of a life that is happier, fuller, and more satisfying than you dreamed was possible!"

No Condemnation

The devil loves when we fall into his traps of sin because he knows that with failures comes condemnation. Condemnation is one of his favorite things. Condemnation is a confidence killer. It robs us of our sense of value and leaves us believing that we are inferior. It is one of the enemy's main tactics to get us stuck and trapped by our past. The devil wants to constantly play reruns in our minds of our biggest failures and greatest moments of regret because he knows that while we watch those reruns, we will feel as though we are never good enough or that our lives have no purpose or meaning. If your thoughts are hurting you and causing you to get down, get a clue. It's not coming from God! Jesus came to destroy the works and plans of Satan, to give hope to the hopeless, and new life to the broken! We serve the God of the great turn around. Rather than being controlled by our feelings, we can live lives of faith knowing that the beautiful, heart-satisfying plans our Father God has for us do not include guilt or regret.

Our sin and our mistakes do not alter our value or disqualify us from running the race that God has for us because His gifts and His callings are without repentance, and He never changes His mind about those to whom He sends His call (Romans 11:29). That means that no matter what we have done or where we have been, God is more interested in the current condition of our hearts than He is in the mistakes of yesterday.

If you have fallen in the past but today your heart is burning with a desire to please God, your past sins do not have to stop you from living life with freedom and joy. Jesus makes all things new and His precious blood has the power to cleanse us and purify our consciences. Your mind does not have to be a place of torment and shame, rather, it was intended to be a place of peace. Condemnation is not a part of God's plan for your life. God's plan is for you to move forward. Declare like the Apostle Paul, "This one thing I do, forgetting what is behind and reaching forward to what is ahead, I press on!"

Revelation 12:11 says, "And they overcame him by the blood of the Lamb, and by the word of their testimony" (KJV). Jesus' blood is greater than our sin and His love is bigger than our past. However, we must declare by faith what the blood of Jesus freely provides for us if we want to move forward with the freedom that Jesus intends for you to have. When we boldly open up our mouth to speak out what God says about us, we shut the door to the enemy and his tools of shame and regret. Declare who that blood has made you to be. Take the freshness that is found in Jesus. You are new creation. You are a child of the King. You have a future full of hope. You are loved by God.

Abandon the concept that you need to struggle to make a good impression, to fit into this little rigid box of "this is who I'm supposed to be and this is what I have to look like and this is how I have to act." Get rid of that religious box once and for all, quit hiding, stop pretending to have it all together, pull off the covers, kick the boxes out from under the bed and just be honest with your Father God. He just wants you to be real with Him.

We live in a world where it can be a struggle to be ourselves, and sometimes we carry that same fear and intimidation over into our relationship with God. It's easy to allow those same insecurities to create a barrier that keeps us from really getting to know the beauty and honesty of God and His great grace.

Sometimes we think that God only has time for "good" people and we think we have to be this stifled, religious version of ourselves in order to be accepted by Him. However, nothing could be further from the truth. He created you to be you. Why would He want you to be anyone else around Him? He wants the real you. He doesn't want you to feel intimidated, like you aren't good enough to come to Him, not important enough for Him to be interested in your life or have time for you. He doesn't want guilt and condemnation to kill your confidence to come to Him. Rather, He wants you to desert every hindrance and run without an ounce of shame or hesitation into His open arms of love.

Going back to the story of the woman caught in the act of adultery, put yourself in her sandals and just imagine how vulnerable she must have felt in that moment. Smack dab in the middle of her sin and shame, she was placed before Jesus. In the midst of accusations, finger pointing, and the gossip of the city, her weakness was fully exposed. She'd been made a public spectacle, disgraced and humiliated her family and disappointed herself. The covers were taken off, she'd been brought out of hiding, stripped of any covering in broad daylight so her weakness and shame were fully exposed.

What Others Think

This is the way I see it. Everyone around her gave her a title. A word didn't have to be spoken, you could just sense that she was the type of girl others saw as inferior, dirty, and unwanted. Nobody saw her as valuable. Because of her actions, nobody considered her worthy of even taking another breath. With accusations constantly attacking her identity from every angle, I guarantee those thoughts began to infiltrate her perception of herself.

Without a doubt, the opinions of others began to influence her sense of self-worth as a well of personal shame and disappointment grew deeper. We, like the condemned woman, also often let the opinions of others become our reality. We try to convince ourselves that what others say doesn't affect us. We try to ignore the brokenness, loneliness, and disappointment we experience, covering it up with empty, lifeless distractions. However, try as we might, nothing we attempt in our own strength can ever take that shame or fill that void.

Do not allow the opinions of others to create perimeters for your life and identity. Instead, allow the anointing of the Word and the power of your own voice destroy those limitations. Do not allow mental strongholds, wrong thoughts, or a distorted self-perception to keep you bound as a prisoner to your past. Jesus came to break every bondage of the enemy and to set the captives free.

With condemnation coming at this precious woman from every direction, what reason would she have to expect any other reaction from the holiest one of all, Jesus? How often have we found ourselves there in our own lives? The world tries to identify us based on the things we have gone through in our past. It can be so natural to allow personal shame to create a false, ungodly self-image.

Despite the various tags your past has tried to attach to you, Jesus wants to redeem your identity. There is freedom in Him. Right in the middle of our uncovered shame and exposed sin, He wants to heal our hearts. Jesus is the lifter of our heads. His healing love is greater than any pain and His grace is stronger than shame. There is no shame that is too great or wound that is too deep. The precious blood of Jesus is stronger than any sin.

When Jesus spoke, one by one, the woman's accusers left her. Once Jesus was left alone with the woman, He spoke to her heart and transformed her life. Alone, without the accusations and distractions of the world, every trace of shame disappeared. Alone, away from the noise and without the barrier of false identities, Jesus was able to tell her that He did not condemn her.

Jesus will meet you in the very spot the accuser had set up to destroy your confidence, your self-image, and your self-worth. If you will run to God in the midst of your shame, the peace of His presence will erase every accusation the enemy designed to destroy your future. The words of Jesus contain the power to silence every lie, lifting you out of shame and into grace.

His acceptance and love will take away every fear and intimidation. The precious blood of Jesus that was shed for you will purge your conscience. His blood speaks as a constant, victorious reminder that you will not be remembered for that. You will not be remembered as unwanted, adulterous, damaged goods, or abandoned. He will propel you out of the pit and into the palace, revealing your true identity as an overcomer.

Jesus took the most unlikely girl in the most unlikely situation and turned around an event that the devil intended to be her destruction. Instead, God used it as a platform to display His love. He honored her with His tender attention, care, and love. In the midst of her shame, He empowered her to move forward. He saved her and her future. She is no longer remembered as an adulterous woman, but as the woman Jesus poured His love upon and gave a second chance. Jesus was not too busy for her. He did not treat her as though she was unworthy to be in His presence. He did not view her as a waste of time or a hopeless cause. His love without condemnation revitalized and created a new identity for her. He wants to do the same for us. We only have to come to Him.

The truth is I am completely fed up with just hearing about or talking about God but not knowing Him for myself. I don't want to get so caught up in the busyness of life and doing things for God that I'm not spending time each and every day getting to know Him more and thriving in the freedom of His love. Sure, we can all go on existing — trying to fill that void in our lives by covering up our brokenness with busyness — but the brokenness will never heal. That busyness is like a Band-Aid: it never heals, it just covers it up the wound.

We find out who we truly are when we get alone with him. His truth silences the accusations of the past and the opinions of others. When we come to Jesus with transparency, honesty, and vulnerability, He can set our feet on solid ground. As we look to Him, we find out how complete we are in Him. The more of His beauty we discover, the more our own identity is revealed. The more we look to Him, the more we see who we are. His love takes the blinders off. His grace melts the masks we use to try to be something or somebody we are not. It's in that place that we are changed. Whatever He says goes and what He believes about us creates our beliefs. Where we have been does not have to dictate where we are going. God is not condemning us or holding us back, so let's not hold ourselves back.

When you are alone, just you and Jesus, everything can change. Without the distractions of the world telling you who you are, He can truly touch your life and mend the broken pieces to make you brand new. Let Him restore your life. Let Him restore your soul. Let Him restore your joy. Let Him restore your love for yourself. Let His love uncover your worth and show you who you truly are.

CHAPTER 7

SEE AND SAY WHAT GOD SEES AND SAYS

O n my way to wholeness, God took me on a wonderful journey where He not only poured out His love upon me in a fresh way, but He also taught me to value myself. He helped change the way I see myself and is still daily helping me become more comfortable in my own skin. Your Father God wants to do the same thing for you. He made you special. There is no one else like you and He longs for your soul to thrive within the freedom of His love.

See

One thing God encouraged me to do during my time of healing was write a list of the things that make me unique — talents and characteristics of my personality that made me one of a kind. Believe me when I tell you that at first, this was really hard. I was at a place where I literally could not think of one thing. I remember just sitting on my bed, pen in hand and an empty sheet of paper in my lap. However, I remained patient with myself, and the Holy Spirit helped me. He reminded me of traits that I didn't think were anything special or even worth mentioning. He pointed out things about me and my personality that maybe I saw as flaws or weaknesses, but He viewed as strengths. He showed me that those things made me special and unique, and that He wanted to use them to highlight His grace upon my life.

We often have no problem esteeming others. Well, let's not stop there. It's time for us to also esteem ourselves. It's time to start picking out the good things about ourselves! Beating ourselves down is not humility. Being hard on ourselves does not please God. He has no part or pleasure in our condemnation.

You are God's creation. It is flat out rude to look at God's perfect creation and tear it apart. You are irreplaceable. You are not your past mistakes. You are not the negative things people have called you. You, the real you, is designed by God and cleansed by the blood of Jesus! You are perfect and complete in Him.

I encourage you to do the same thing I did. Take the time to write out a list of things that make you unique, and keep it before your eyes. I understand that it can be so easy to constantly emphasize the negative in your life. If we are not careful, almost subconsciously, we point out our flaws. However, it is time to focus on the positive things. This may require significant effort, but you must change your focus to experience change in your life.

God will help you by showing you things about yourself that He specifically designed, things that make you, you. Think about those things. Value your uniqueness. If you are a little quirky, that's okay; we all are — it's what makes life fun! Learn to laugh at yourself and love yourself. I don't believe God intended for us to constantly take ourselves so seriously. Instead, He wants us to take His love seriously. Go ahead and look at a picture of yourself and instead of automatically tearing yourself apart, change directions and notice the beauty God has given you. Sometimes we just have to practice being positive and retrain the way you think about ourselves.

Be a friend — a real friend — to yourself by being patient with yourself. Many times, I have been tempted to feel frustrated with myself because I still felt stuck. I soon realized that if my best friend was going through a similar experience, I would not beat her down. I wouldn't look at her in disgust and ask, "Shouldn't you be over this already!?" No, I would do everything within my power to encourage her and let her know that I believe in her. Well, it's time to encourage and believe in yourself. This is only the beginning – you are going to end in victory. Give yourself a second chance. As long as you don't quit, as long as you keep putting one foot in front of the other, you have a guaranteed victory! God will complete what He started in your life.

I am convinced you will be completely amazed when you think about how uniquely God made you and take the time to actually write those things down. But then you need to take another step and speak those traits out loud.

Say

Did you know that it is absolutely impossible to be thankful and depressed at the same time? I have never met a depressed, thankful person. Thanksgiving and depression are like oil and water. Try as hard as you possibly can, they will never mix. So once you've thought of your strengths, don't quit there. Thank God out loud for making you so unique. Hope and joy accompany thankful hearts, and God wants you to be happy being you.

The quickest way to escape a pity party is to start thanking God! Right where you are, right now, begin to thank God for investing all He is in you. He poured out His heart when He created you, designing every detail of your personality. You are fearfully and wonderfully made! You are made in the very likeness and image of your Father! Your life is not an accident or a mere coincidence. This world is far better because you are in it. You are not the mistakes you have made. You are not a waste of space. You have a matchless beauty and an endless worth. Think about those things that make you one of a kind and write them down. Then speak those things out. Life and death is in the power of the tongue. Use your mouth to release life.

The more we declare what God says about us, the more we will see how much Jesus loves us and how freely He has forgiven us. His freedom empowers us to forgive ourselves. God did not remember me for my failures and I became determined to not remember myself for those things. I am not my divorce. I am not my failures. I am not the pain I have caused others. No matter what you are facing, no matter what you have done in the past, nothing can separate you from God's amazing love. His love is bigger than your past, bigger than your sin, and greater than your failures! God is on your side, no matter what. He will never stop cheering you on and believing in you.

That means if you have become caught in a downward spiral of despair and have found yourself in an unhealthy place, it is not too late for you. Choose life! Choose to focus on the positive.

People who know they are loved and chosen by God are fearless. Loving yourself and valuing the person God made you to be carries with it a boldness that is beautiful and a freedom you cannot get anywhere else. The Bible tells you that you can be transformed by the renewing of your mind (Romans 12:2). The Word of God has more than enough power to transform every single thing about your life, including the way you see yourself.

By speaking out what God says about you, your mind will be renewed to see yourself the way He does. As you get ready for each day, say, "God loves me and I love myself! He is on my side and something good is going to happen to me today!" Get your hopes up high and watch God rock your world and do superabundantly above and beyond anything you could hope, dream, or imagine!

As I mentioned in chapter 5, I used to be so ashamed to look at myself in a mirror. Although it was not easy at first, instead of hanging my head low, I now purposely march myself to the biggest mirror I can find, look myself square in the eyes, smile from ear to ear, point at myself, and joyfully declare, "*You* are beautiful. *You* are loved by God. *You* are unique. *You* love people. *You* are radiant with life and with the joy of the Lord. *You* are special. There is no one else like *you*." Then I go on and speak out those things I have written on my list of unique qualities. I have found that the more I speak this way, the more I believe it and if I believe it, I will speak it.

There is so much power in our words. Our words can change our world around us. Our words even contain the power to change the way we feel about ourselves. The reflection in my mirror that once stirred up so much pain within me, now causes me to smile. Joy floods my heart as I declare who God has created me to be and I boldly say, "I will not be remembered for that!"

You may walk around with your head hung low because the devil tries to weigh you down with his shame and guilt. But Jesus is the lifter of your head! He wants you to live life with your shoulders back and your head lifted high. Your Father desires for your eyes to radiate with hope and for your soul to shine with a confidence that only comes from Him.

So put a smile on your face and remind yourself how special God made you. If we only knew what takes place when we are bold enough to speak out what God says about us, we would want to do it all the time. Our words carry so much power and authority. Like the steering wheel on a car, we can use our mouth to direct our lives. If you don't like the direction your life has been going, grab ahold of the steering wheel by opening up your mouth. Change the direction of your life by changing the words you speak.

In other words, if you want the dog, quit calling the cat! Declare by faith what you want and thank God that you have it. Smile at yourself in the mirror and declare with joy that you love God, you love yourself, and you love others! Start saying that you are happy to be you.

Full Flavor

Ephesians 4:29 says, "Let no foul or polluting language, nor evil word nor unwholesome or worthless talk [ever] come out of your mouth, but only such [speech] as is good and beneficial to the spiritual progress of others, as is fitting to the need and the occasion, that it may be a blessing and give grace (God's favor) to those who hear it." Not only should this verse guide the way we speak to others, it should also guide the way we speak to ourselves. We must speak positive things and think good thoughts about ourselves.

When you speak the living Word, the way you're living changes. The more you say what God says about you, the more real His love will become. Joshua 1:8 says, "This Book of the Law shall not depart out of your mouth, but you shall meditate on it day and night . . . . For then you shall make your way prosperous, and then you shall deal wisely and have good success."

When the Bible mentions "meditating on the Word," it is referring to actively setting your mind upon what God says and then speaking it out loud to yourself. I've heard one minister relate meditating on the Word to taking a tea bag and immersing it in a cup of hot water. Imagine what would happen if you were to take a tea bag, dip it in the water, and then immediately take it out? The flavor in the tea bag would not have the opportunity to permeate the liquid. However, if you took that same tea bag and let it sit in the hot water for 10 or 15 minutes, then stir it around, the richness of the tea would saturate that water, and the water would be completely transformed.

In the same way, there is a drastic difference between skimming over a scripture about how much God loves you and taking that exact same verse and allowing it to saturate the core of your being, transforming you by the renewing of your mind. The Bible is nourishment for your spirit and strength for your soul. As you mediate upon the Word of God and speak it to yourself, you allow His words to digest and become a part of who you are.

Jesus said His words are spirit and they are life (John 6:63). The Word of God is alive and full of power, active, operative, and energizing. His Truth is sharper than any two-edged sword and has the ability to separate our souls from the pain of our past. Each word is drenched in His anointing. Speaking His Words of freedom cuts off every chain of bondage. One word from God has more than enough power to completely transform our lives and change the way we see ourselves. However it is when we speak it that we release the power that is within the Word

Scripture is God-breathed. As we speak it out loud, we release the power and life that is within each word to set us free from anything that is not of God as His love illuminates our hearts. As the Holy Spirit works with the truth that we continually speak, the torment of the devil is cut off from the roots to wither and die. The Holy Spirit will separate us from the dead things of our past and empower us to move forward with boldness, no longer weighed down by insecurities.

Trust that the Holy Spirit is working alongside the Word, using that truth you are speaking to strengthen your heart and cleanse your soul from the pain of your past. Direct the Word like an arrow to help you in your specific situation. Trust God and thank Him that as you speak a specific scripture, you are being consecrated, which means to be set-apart. Believe that God's Word sets you apart from depression, sets you apart from those unhealthy soul ties, and sets you apart from that pain from your past. Let His opinions and great love become the essence of what makes you, *you.*

Allow the richness His Word to completely saturate your heart and become the anchor of your soul. Stir yourself up with His truth and enjoy the full flavor of His marvelous freedom!

CHAPTER 8

FORGIVE

There is not much God can do within a hard, doubting, rebellious heart. Yet forgiveness is a wonderful heart-softener. It truly is a beautiful thing. When we choose to forgive, miracles happen. Our hearts become available and open towards God and it gives Him the opportunity to heal our deepest wounds. Forgiveness positions us for healing and freedom.

First Yourself

I believe that soul freedom often begins with forgiveness, and that forgiveness must, many times, be directed towards our own selves. When the truth that we are already loved and forgiven by our Father God becomes a reality in our hearts, we are empowered to release ourselves. Choosing to forgive is choosing to live free. God does not expect nor require us to be perfect, so we should quit demanding perfection of ourselves.

The Bible says that the precious blood of Jesus can purge a guilty conscience (Hebrews 10:22). You can live free of the burden of condemnation. Regret does not have to define your life. Your Father God wants to give you a fresh start and a clean slate, but He needs you to cooperate.

God is not holding a grudge against you, and He doesn't want you to hold a grudge against yourself. Clinging to your mistakes and constantly rehashing the ways you have let others down will only work death in your soul. Jesus came to give you life! It is time for you to get a new, heavenly perspective. God sees you as spotless and clean in the blood of Jesus; it's time to see yourself that way.

I understand how difficult it can be to forgive yourself. At times, it's easier to let go of the things others have done than to let go of your own mistakes. It's difficult when you see all the hurt you have caused and the people you have disappointed. I am far too acquainted with the misery of living under the belief that you are a failure and don't deserve forgiveness.

However, strength comes from knowing that God has not cast you aside or given up hope. He believes in you. Regardless of your past, your Father is not ashamed of you. He is on your side and He wants you to forgive yourself, live without shame, and love who you are in Him.

The only way to do this is by faith. Faith, which is of the heart, helps you let go of the things behind you. When we do something by faith, we do it by fully relying on God. Faith takes you out of the confinement of your ability and into God's unlimited power and resources! You can simply say, "By faith, I am choosing to let go of the pain of my past and I choose to forgive myself today." Second Corinthians 10:5 tells us that by speaking words of faith, you can cast down any contradictory imagination and take every thought captive to the obedience of Christ.

However, we can have faith in our heart and still have doubt come across our mind. So no matter what contradictory thoughts run across your mind vying for your attention, by faith choose to forgive yourself. Regardless of your feelings, choose to be happy with yourself. The just shall live by faith, not by feelings and reasonings.

When doubt comes across your mind and you start rehashing the past, wondering whether or not you are really forgiven, remember faith is of the heart. Thoughts of doubt are not problems as long as you stand firm in your place of believing.

When we stop pushing the rewind button in our minds, we can see the new thing God is wanting to do. We can let go of the pain of our past and release ourselves from the wrong decisions we have made. We are not our failures. We are not the pain we may have caused others. We have a worth that is irreversible and a value that knows no end. When our Creator looks at us, He doesn't see our mistakes, He sees us and loves us with everything that He is.

Be an imitator of God and follow His example. It is time to leave the past in the past and give yourself a clean slate. Jesus has given you a fresh start. Now, He is simply waiting for you to leave it all behind and enjoy the freedom of His everlasting mercies. Love yourself and forgive yourself the way your Father does. Your best days are just ahead!

Then Others

God doesn't stop at just empowering you to forgive yourself. He will also strengthen you to forgive those who have hurt you.

I'm telling you, we *want* to forgive other people. I understand how easy it can be to think, "After the way that person treated us, they don't deserve forgiveness." We think we are getting even with the person who has hurt us by holding a grudge. However, the only person we hurt is ourselves. I'm not saying you do not have valid reasons to feel hurt or hold a grudge. At one time or another, we all face the temptation to grow bitter. Yet resentment will keep us from a life of peace and victory.

I thank God for Rick Renner's book, *You Can Get Over It*. The biblical wisdom he shares has helped me let go of bitterness and experience greater freedom in my soul. Rick said, "Whatever we meditate on will take root and produce fruit in our lives. Therefore, we have to constantly be on guard regarding what we allow to dominate our thoughts. God doesn't allow us to justify bitterness in our hearts just because we've been wronged or because we have a 'good reason.' Those so-called 'reasons' are simply traps — designed to hinder or destroy us if we allow them to remain lodged in our minds where they can grow and eventually dominate our thoughts. When we're wounded by some sort of offense, that wound will fester if we leave it unchecked. We must determine to let go of that offense and move forward."

The way I see it, we can either hold on to all of our reasons why a person doesn't deserve our forgiveness and hold on to our right to be bitter, or we can let it all go and grab ahold of freedom. Life is happier when lived with a forgiving heart!

Unforgiveness Isn't Worth It

The old saying goes, "Unforgiveness is the poison we drink hoping another will die." Nothing corrodes a life and keeps us chained like a bitter heart. That is exactly why Satan tries so hard to get us caught in a web of resentment. Unforgiveness comes straight from the pit of hell and works death. It clouds our minds and affects each area of our lives. Resentment robs us of our future by keeping us stuck in the quicksand of the past.

A bitter heart also makes you easy prey for Satan who wants to keep you trapped in his prison of unforgiveness, unable to defend yourself against attacks. Unforgiveness spreads like a disease, eats away at your soul, drains you of your strength, cuts you off from peace, and drowns you in despair, torment and confusion.

Dear friends, do not view unforgiveness as an unavoidable part of life, but see it as the deadly trap it is. The darkness and death that accompany grudges is a foretaste of hell. Why would we ever want to open our hearts to such destruction? Why would we give the devil such free reign to wreak havoc within our souls?

Why go on tasting hell when Jesus wants to give you heaven on earth? Shake off the past and let go of the pain. Rehashing the past keeps you stuck, but forgiveness leads you forward. Past wounds do not have to fester and eat away at your soul. You do not have to be paralyzed by the pain of rejection and disappointment. Jesus has opened up the prison door and has provided the way out and the power to live free. There is light at the end of the tunnel, and that glorious light will lead you out. No matter where you may be in life today, Jesus guarantees that it is never too late for you.

First Corinthians 10:13 says, "No temptation has overtaken you except such as is common to man; but God is faithful, who will not allow you to be tempted beyond what you are able, but with the temptation will also make the way of escape, that you may be able to bear it" (NKJV). What wonderful news! Regardless of how strong the temptation to yield to resentment may be, God promises He will always make a way of escape! We no longer have to live under the load of bitterness, stuck in a prison of unforgiveness. We can choose freedom. As Rick Renner puts it, "You are the only one who can choose to walk away from these deadly attitudes." Forgiveness will separate your soul from torment, loose you from the pain of isolation, and position your heart for breakthrough.

You can do what Mark 11:25 says, "If you have anything against anyone, forgive him and let it drop (leave it, let it go)." With the help of the Holy Spirit, you can loose yourself and others from the bondage of resentment. The choice is up to you. Do you want to live trapped, or do you want to live free? When we delay forgiveness, we postpone our own freedom. Don't keep yourself from the life of peace and liberty available to you. Let go of every grudge. The forgiving life is the happy life.

CHAPTER 9

HAPPY NOW

Being content and happy with who you are is one of the most appealing qualities a person can have. The fearlessness of a woman who knows she does not have to be anything she is not, or the unwavering confidence of a man standing firm in his self-worth is absolutely captivating! Stay true to the personality God gave you. You will never be happy if you are always trying to be who you think other people want or expect you to be. Live authentically without any chains or confinements. Just be you in your rawest form and enjoy your uniqueness!

Constant Versus Change

When our value is wrapped up in things that change, we live on the verge of crisis. If our sense of worth is based on things such as our appearance, our career, or our relationship status, we are living on sinking sand because everything in this world has the potential to crumble in an instant. Our perception of our worth will always fluctuate when it is based on anything other than Jesus. We will live a roller coaster life, going up and down, ruled by our ever-changing emotions and situations. The only thing that will be constant is our own inconsistency. Let me tell you from experience, this is definitely not a satisfying way to live. God did not intend for self-worth to fluctuate. He desires we have stable and secure lives rooted deep in His affection. I love roller coasters, but I certainly do not want to live my life on one!

On one of the most pitiful days of my life (and believe me, I've had many to choose from), I texted one of my best friends and simply said, "I'm so pathetic." Not even four hours later, I texted her again, this time saying, "Oh my gosh, I'm so happy!" I remember laughing hysterically at myself after sending that last message, realizing I had done a complete 180 in just a few hours. I ended up writing these words in my journal: "Olivia! Olivia! *Please* promise me that next time, you WILL NOT listen to your feelings! Feelings change! Feelings are fickle! Feelings can lie to you and be really, really ridiculous! Please don't listen to them! Save yourself from pathetic days and listen to Jesus."

Then, glancing through my journal, I noticed that, just a few pages before, I had written a similar warning for myself and forgotten all about it! It was then I realized that if I'm not going to allow my feelings to run my life, I constantly need to remind myself of who I truly am.

What enabled me to go from zero to 60 was that smack dab in the middle of my pity party, the thought came to me, "What if I just made the decision to learn to be happy right now?" Right now. Before anything changes. With everything exactly the way it is — while I am single, feeling alone, before all my dreams come to pass. I decided to learn to be happy right then so that later on, when more of my dreams had come to pass, I would know that my happiness was not based on those things. I would have the confidence of knowing I had learned to be content no matter what stage of life I might find myself in.

Paul said in Philippians 4:11–12, "Not that I am implying that I was in any personal want, for I have learned how to be content (satisfied to the point where I am not disturbed or disquieted) in whatever state I am. I know how to be abased and live humbly in straitened circumstances, and I know how to enjoy plenty and live in abundance. I have learned in any and all circumstances the secret of facing every situation." That means that right now, right where we are, we can be satisfied, fulfilled, and enjoy the beauty of today.

I have often found myself in the trap of either looking off into the future, putting so much emphasis on how great "one day" will look, or looking back, reminiscing about how special "back then" was. To be honest, this is still something I struggle with at times. Yet I am tired of the constant ping-pong game, being bounced from place to place, event to event, looking to those things for a sense of satisfaction. Any fulfillment I receive from that kind of thinking is only temporary. I love to dream about the future, yet I am determined not to let right now fall through my fingertips.

Let's no longer live in the trap of always thinking the grass is greener on the other side; we have a lot of great grass to work with right in front of us! There is no event, relationship, or accomplishment that has the power to permanently sustain and fulfill us. You can be married and depressed just like you can be single and depressed. You can be on vacation and be depressed just like you can be at work and be depressed. If we are always looking to things or events to satisfy us, we will be looking all of our lives and constantly missing out on what today has to offer.

We have the power to control our thoughts and words. As we think the right thoughts, speak the right words, and choose to stay thankful, we will learn to be happy, just content in whatever season we are in. Jesus is the source of our joy and He is always the same, regardless of what does or does not change in our lives. Before we live out all of our dreams, before we are in a relationship, before that vacation, before we reach our desired body shape, before we get that new job, or before anything else, we can just be happy NOW. Like Paul, we can learn to be happy and content no matter what season of life we find ourselves in.

Joy in Imperfection

The life of a perfectionist is exhausting. Ask me how I know? I've dealt with being a perfectionist throughout my life. Not only is it hard for anyone else to be enough for you, but you will never be enough for yourself. Don't even get me started describing what happens when things do not go perfectly as planned! If you are postponing your happiness, waiting for the perfect life, let me tell you what personal experience has taught me: you will be waiting a long, long time!

Besides, perfection is overrated. Even God is not looking for perfect people with perfect lives. If you think about people in the Bible, the ones God used were not those who never got knocked down or lived lives free from trials. He used those who would simply trust Him enough to allow Him to do something beautiful in their lives.

Joseph's life was far from perfect. He was sold into slavery by his own brothers, thrown into a pit, and later imprisoned. However, he kept believing that somehow, some way, God's favor would turn around what the devil meant for evil. As a result of this belief, Joseph watched God do the impossible in his life. Eventually he was honored by Pharaoh and put second in command over all of Egypt. God can always take that mess in your life and transform it by His grace. He will restore your soul and give you beauty for ashes!

When we postpone happiness, waiting to first reach a certain goal or accomplishment, we live miserable, empty, defeated lives. We delay joy and put off being satisfied with ourselves. Don't postpone your joy until after your prison sentence is done. Don't wait to realize your value until after you lose that weight. There is life to be lived right now. Before we can genuinely enjoy our lives, we have to be happy with ourselves. We can love ourselves on each step of the journey.

I had to learn to quit living against myself and just be at peace with myself. So maybe my body doesn't look the way it did last year. Am I going to be miserable until I'm back to my "perfect" shape? Am I going to allow the scale to determine my value for that day? So I'm not where I expected to be at this age. Perhaps I expected to have accomplished more. Am I going to beat myself down about it? No!

In the midst of every possible imperfection, regardless of what you may be facing, choose to be happy right now! Be comfortable in your own skin and rely on the Father's help to find joy in simply being you. In His strength, love yourself and be patient with yourself.

CHAPTER 10

A NEW DAY

A man was walking past an elephant at a circus and noticed the elephant was tied to a small stake by a thin rope around his leg. The man could not understand why such a massive, powerful animal did not simply snap the rope and break free from his confinement. Out of curiosity, he asked the elephant trainer how a little rope could keep such a strong creature in place. The trainer explained that when the elephant was very young (and much smaller), they had used a similar rope to keep him bound. At that age, the small rope was enough to hold him. As the elephant grew, he became conditioned to think he could not break away. The elephant came to believe the rope could still hold him, so he never tried to break free.

The man was amazed. Although the elephant could break loose at any time, he did not even try to escape. The elephant had grown accustomed to believing the rope was stronger than he was, and so he stayed stuck right there. This powerful, gigantic creature was allowing past memories and a wrong mindset to limit his present abilities.

The devil wants to persuade you that you can never go beyond where you have been. He will desperately try to get you to believe the lies that it is too difficult to move forward and life will never be the same again. Perhaps when you look over your life, you think, "There has never been a time in my life when I thought I was exceptional. I've never liked my personality. I've never truly loved myself." Or you may think, "I've always dealt with that insecurity. I've always been intimidated by others and trapped in the cycle of comparison. I've always felt unwanted."

Well, here is the good news: today is a new day! Even if you are used to living in that bondage of believing lies and you feel as though you have been stuck in the same place year after year, today is your fresh start! Jesus has flung open wide the prison door and you are no longer a captive! You do not have to keep going around in circles, stuck in that old, dead place of being harassed by your past. Life does not have to keep being like it's always been. It doesn't matter if you never realized your worth and you have allowed your past to define you. Today can be the day you start living free and learning to be happy being you.

Let's give up the "elephant mindset." Why should we go on allowing negative experiences and failures to shape our lives and hold us back? Why should we live bound to what has happened when our best days are right in front of us?

Hebrews 3:7–8 says to us, "Therefore, as the Holy Spirit says: Today, if you will hear His voice, do not harden your hearts." Today is a new day. Today is your fresh start. Hear your Father's voice saying that He loves you and He knows the plans He has for you! Don't harden your heart by doubting or rebelling against what He says about you. Heed, surrender, and give yourself over to Him and His amazing love for you. Don't offer your wrists and allow the enemy to handcuff you to your past by dwelling on self-limiting thoughts; willingly present yourself to Jesus! Come to Him without fear and let Him heal your heart with His unending love.

Leave that mental prison cell. Shake off the dust. Allow the Father to put His robe of honor around you, sandals on your feet, and a ring on your finger. In the midst of your shame, He will honor you with His love. Jesus removes every burden, empowering you to move forward with your shoulders back and your head lifted up without fear.

In this moment, wherever you may be, hear what God is saying about you and then agree with Him! Don't put it off. Why postpone your freedom and your joy when it belongs to you right now? Each day matters. What we do every day adds up and makes a difference in our lives.

Shame cannot stand in His presence, and the power that is within you is much stronger than the chains that have tried to bind you! Don't live like that elephant, stuck in the same place. Whom the Son has set free is free indeed!

God's mercies are brand new every morning and His covenant with you will never be removed. Nothing can drive a wedge between you and His undying affection. Let Your Father crown you with His mercy and cover you with His love. See Him pointing you out of the crowd as He joyfully calls you "Child." You are the one He has always wanted.

Remember, your life is a result of the story that you choose to believe about yourself. The elephant believed he could not break loose from that small rope, so he never even tried to. Our believing and our speaking have the power to change our lives. Think positive thoughts about yourself and choose to love yourself today. Don't let a day pass by without the water of God's

Word refreshing your soul, preventing hardness from setting in and overtaking your heart.

Scrubbing the Pot

I am a big oatmeal eater. To me, there's nothing like a hearty, hot bowl of oats mixed with chopped apples, walnuts, and cinnamon to kick off a day. However, I've quickly discovered that if I do not immediately put some water in the pot after cooking my breakfast, the residue of those leftover oats harden and become difficult to remove. The longer those oats sat there, the harder it is. When I've been in a rush and left the dirty pot sitting on the stovetop all day, you can imagine how long and hard I had to scrub to get the pot clean.

In the same way, the longer we listen to the lies of Satan, the harder it is to get those lies out. Just like with the leftover oatmeal, his lies attach themselves and harden in your heart. His aim is to keep you stuck in the past, doubting that God will do anything great in your life. A hard heart is an unbelieving heart. However, remember that your believing is the very thing that allows God to do the impossible in your life.

So how can you guard your heart from the hardness of doubt? Put the water of God's Word on it! Combat the lies and shame of the devil with the washing of the water of the Word!

The Choice Is up to You

I remember exactly where I was when, as a teenager, the Holy Spirit spoke these words to my heart: "It is a choice to rejoice." Years later, I continue to realize there is so much truth within that one statement. Every single day, the choice is up to us. Life and death are both set before us. We can choose to dwell on the lies that the thief will bring to us or we can choose to follow our Good Shepherd. Choose life! Choose joy! Make the daily decision that you are simply going to learn to be happy with you.

Decide to love yourself right now, love your imperfect self right in the midst of your imperfect life. That's right! Go ahead and be bold enough to love yourself in the midst of your imperfections. Celebrate who God made you to be even if you're smack dab in the middle of your failures. Don't wait to measure up or feel like you are enough. You will never be enough for your ever-changing feelings.

It is a choice to rejoice. Be happy with where you are and say, "I'm okay and I'm on my way!" Do not give yourself the option to give up. God believes in you, so believe in yourself. God does not hold any grudges against you and neither should you. God has freely forgiven you, now it is time to forgive yourself. God is happy with you!

Loose yourself from the chains of resentment. Let bitterness out and let the Healer in. Forgive and live free. Refuse to remember yourself by your failures or the things people have done to you. No more shackles, no more chains — you are free. You are in control of what you think about yourself, so choose to be happy being you because you are loved and you will not be remembered for that. You can love who God has created you to be!

PART THREE

Moving
Forward

CHAPTER 11

WHICH WAY TO GO

Rerouting

Faithful is He who has called you and He is faithful to do it. God will complete what He has started and take you to the finish line, right on time!

This truth became alive to me soon after my divorce. It was one of my first days on the job nannying a little boy, and I needed to drive him to his therapy class. Somehow I got on the wrong highway, and ended up in an unfamiliar neighborhood. Time was ticking away. The dread of being late and the worry of not knowing where I was caused me to become frantic. I think it is safe to say that I may have freaked out a little. Just to make it clear, by "may have," I mean I definitely did freak out, and by "a little," I mean I freaked out a whole lot. Although getting lost isn't a rare occurrence for me, in this instance, it was bad. And if I say it was bad, trust me, it was *really* bad.

However, if you have ever driven with a GPS, you know there is one word that can set your racing heart at rest, ease your soul, and change everything in an instant: *Rerouting*! That one word brings a deep sigh of relief because you know everything is going to be okay.

That day in the car, the Spirit of God ministered so vividly to my heart. He reminded me that if a man-made global positioning system could get me where I was supposed to be, my Heavenly Father could do the same thing and so much more! Something was ignited on the inside of me, and I realized right then that God is far greater and much more merciful than any GPS system!

The same is true for you. God is your Faithful Finisher and He is on your side! He has a route for your life that you haven't thought of. He has a highway for your restoration and success. He knows exactly how to get you from where you are to where you are meant to be. I've heard it said that after every setback, God has great comeback! The One who has called and chosen you knew every failure and mistake you would make — but that didn't faze Him for one second.

There is no need to live uptight about things you cannot change. Stop looking in the rearview mirror. God is greater than what is behind you and has a future waiting that is greater than your past. If you took the wrong road and made some mistakes, don't worry; we all have. Take a deep breath and a sigh of relief; God will get you exactly where you are supposed to be, right on time. The Holy Spirit is rerouting — He knows the path that will get you right back on track! Your failures don't take God by surprise. Your past doesn't faze Him for even a moment, so why let it hinder you? The Greater One is in you and He is stronger than what has happened to you.

He is greater than time and He can restore the years you felt like you lost, leading you on a path of triumph and soul freedom. Just jump on His access ramp of grace and watch Him refresh your life in ways that will far surpass your every expectation.

During a time of prayer, God spoke to my heart and with boldness I began to declare, "I'm right on track and I'm not looking back!" I believe that is for you as well. Stop looking at the time you feel was wasted and believe your greatest days are in front of you. God can redeem the time! He makes all things new!

You have the power to tell your soul what it will focus on. If you don't like the direction your life has been going, just grab a hold of the steering wheel (your tongue), and turn your life in the direction God is leading! You can change the direction of your life by changing the direction of your thoughts and words.

The Help of the Holy Spirit

Time after time, Jesus referred to the Holy Spirit as the Comforter. When Jesus told His disciples that He would be returning to heaven, He said, "However, I am telling you nothing but the truth when I say it is profitable (good, expedient, advantageous) for you that I go away. Because if I do not go away, the Comforter (Counselor, Helper, Advocate, Intercessor, Strengthener, Standby) will not come to you [into close fellowship with you]; but if I go away, I will send Him to you [to be in close fellowship with you]" (John 16:7). When you believe in Jesus and make Him Lord of your life, the Holy Spirit comes to live within you and He is with you always to help you in every area of your life.

The Holy Spirit will prompt you and let you know when a thought is trying to steal from your peace. Follow peace. Let peace rule in your heart. Only allow thoughts to gain access to your soul that sustain rest and joy. In this way, you will be doing what the Bible says, "Above all else, guard and protect your heart because out of it all the issues of life flow (Proverbs 4:23)." You will be guarding your entire life by maintaining a healthy soul and a healthy relationship with yourself. A flourishing, healthy soul leads to a flourishing, healthy life.

If you have ever seen a rapidly moving river, you have probably noticed how sediment, logs, and dirt all get washed away by the current. Rapid rivers cleanse and push out substances that can cause blockage. Whatever does not belong cannot withstand the current. In the same way, the pure, living river of Jesus and His Holy Spirit will powerfully renew, cleanse, purify, and purge your soul. His Spirit and His Word work together. When you take time to pray in the Spirit, you release the powerful rivers of life. Those rivers clear away the dead things of your past. The old is gone and the new has come. Speaking and renewing your mind with the Word of God causes thoughts that did not originate in Jesus to be uprooted and swept away. What marvelous freshness is found in Jesus! He has come to give us a brand new life with an entirely new way of thinking and speaking.

Replace those old thoughts of defeat with God's thoughts of victory. The thief comes to steal, kill, and destroy, but Jesus has come that you might have and enjoy life in abundance! He wants your soul to overflow with life. God is the Healer of the brokenhearted and the Restorer of your soul. Jesus knows the way for you to enjoy liberty every single day. In fact, He is the Way. Will you follow Him? Listen to His opinion of you. Let your soul become alive in His freedom.

Follow the Leader

In the kid's game Follow the Leader, the winner was the one who could follow the leader the best. Well, whoever closely follows our Leader and Shepherd, Jesus, will be a winner in life! Ephesians 5:1 encourages us to be followers of God. The

Amplified Version puts it this way, "Be imitators of God (copy Him and follow His example), as well-beloved children imitate their father." Let's follow the Leader and not miss a single step. Let's think what He thinks, say what He says, and do what He does. He will lead you out of defeat and into victory, out of fear and into peace, out of depression and into joy!

Jesus is the Good Shepherd. Out of pure love, He laid down His life for the sheep to give them new life. Jesus died so that our old selves could die with Him. Jesus has made us brand new. He has taken away our past. The old has gone, the fresh and new has come!

Jesus said, "I give them eternal life, and they shall never lose it" (John 10:28). The life and love that Jesus gives can completely redeem your life from destruction and transform any situation you are dealing with. Nothing can snatch you from the palm of your Father's hand. He is greater than all. He is greater than your failures, greater than your prison cell, and greater than your shame. He has freedom for your soul. God has redeemed you; He has taken you out of the control of darkness and placed you in His kingdom. You are His very own and He has given you authority to set the devil on the run!

Jesus tells you in Luke 10:19 that He has given you authority and nothing shall by any means hurt you. The pain of your past and the lies of the devil cannot shake you. You have been set free by the Truth, anchored in the Solid Rock. You are in control of what you choose to believe. In the light of God's love, see who you truly are. You no longer need to struggle to earn a sense of worth by attempting to be something you are not. You are enough in Jesus!

Let Jesus be the strength of your life. Think and act in line with what your Father says about you. Resist the voice of the stranger. When he calls you ashamed, afraid, and alone, silence his lies by magnifying the voice of your faithful Father. He has picked you out of the crowd and He has called you by a new name. He says, "You are mine! You are loved! You are forgiven!" The new name God has given you propels you forward and empowers you.

I'm captivated when I read in the gospels about how Jesus called His disciples. When Jesus spotted Matthew sitting at a tax collection booth, He didn't see a "repulsive sinner" and try to avoid him. On the contrary, with a heart full of compassion, Jesus looked at him and said, "Follow Me." Without hesitation, Matthew left everything, choosing a new life and a new identity.

One day as Jesus was walking by the Sea of Galilee, He noticed two fishermen throwing their nets into the sea. Jesus called to them, "Follow Me, and I will make you fishers of men." As soon as they heard His call, Peter and his brother, Andrew, abandoned their nets and became His disciples. Not far from where He'd found Peter and Andrew, Jesus saw two other brothers, James and John, mending their nets with their father in their boat. As soon as Jesus' invitation hit their ears, they left their father, their boat, and their nets in order to follow Him.

The wonderful thing about following Jesus is, the moment we choose to go after Him, we leave the past behind! It would have been impossible for Matthew, Peter, or John to follow Jesus and still remain in the tax collection booth, with their nets, or in their boat. Responding to His call required them to leave where they were. One of my favorite worship songs says, "I have decided to follow Jesus. No turning back." One thing is for sure, we can't go in two directions at the same time. Following Jesus means moving forward. The thief will work around the clock, attempting to chain us to our past by calling us by our old name — worthless, forgotten, damaged — but we don't have to accept those old lies. Just like the disciples, we can leave our old identity in the dust. Give no thought to the voice of a stranger; direct your focus to the call of your Good Shepherd. John 10:3 says he calls you by name and leads you out. He *is* calling you by name, saying, "You are loved! You are free! You are forgiven! You are Mine and you are moving forward!"

According to Psalm 23, when the Lord is your Shepherd, you will never lack a thing! He will cause you to rest in fresh, green pastures and lead you beside the still waters. He will restore your soul and guide you along the right paths. Even when you walk through the darkest valleys, there is nothing to fear. He is with you to comfort, protect, and lead you out. Today, Jesus is calling you to follow Him into a brand new life. He will lead you out of brokenness and torment into wholeness and joy. He will restore your soul. Let's leave the old behind and allow the anthem of our lives to become, "I have decided to follow Jesus, no turning back!"

Be bold to follow the Leader, for He knows the way that leads to life.

CHAPTER 12

BE THANKFUL

Bless (affectionately, gratefully praise) the Lord, O my soul; and all that is [deepest] within me, bless His holy name!

2 Bless (affectionately, gratefully praise) the Lord, O my soul, and forget not [one of] all His benefits—

Psalm 103:1–2

It is impossible to stay discouraged when you tell yourself to focus on how faithful God is and everything that He is working out for you. I guarantee you will never meet a thankful, depressed person. You are either one or the other. I promise, you cannot be both. That is why praise is the remedy for all heaviness. Those chains and weights will not remain in your soul if each time a discouraging thought crosses your mind, you begin to open your mouth and boldly declare what God says about you and your life.

One conversation I had with my dad really helped me. I was going through a difficult time dealing with my emotions. I told him that sometimes I felt like a complete hypocrite, sounding so happy and bold when preaching, only to have to continually stir myself up in my private life. My dad told me that I was not living a fake life, I was simply learning how to live by faith. This is where the rubber meets the road. It's one thing to know what to do, but it's another thing to do it. When we give God thanks when we least feel like it, that is faith. In fact, I've found out that the best time to praise God is actually when we least feel like it.

Faith, joy, peace, hope, encouragement, strength — all of these go hand in hand. That means that when we are feeling weak, hopeless, and depressed, we can speak the opposite of how we feel and stir up joy by encouraging ourselves in the Lord.

When circumstances attempt to steal your joy, go ahead and put on the garment of praise instead of a heavy, burdened, and failing spirit. I promise you, praise looks a whole lot better on you than heaviness does! And there is no heaviness that is stronger than the praise that is in you. When the darkness and depression of the devil try to attach themselves to you, praise is your spiritual PAM® Spray that gives you a non-stick coating! This is the key to keeping shame off and joy on. This is how we live stable lives of consistent victory.

As we keep our minds stayed on Jesus, He will keep us in perfect peace. We can trust Him. Do not forget any of His benefits. Remind yourself how good God is to you. Talk about how He has never failed you and He never will. Be thankful and say so to Him.

I love how different translations of Psalm 103:5 point out that God wants to satisfy your desires with good things. The NLT says, "He fills my life with good things!" He will satisfy you and restore your life in ways more fulfilling than you could ever imagine. As the Amplified version highlights, He will richly satisfy not only your necessity, but also your desires at your personal age and situation. He is a personal God who knows you intimately. He is faithful to bring to pass the secret desires of your heart. Whole hearts and fulfilled desires are a part of His wonderful plan of restoration for you.

Psalm 103 vividly illustrates your Father's abundant, individual, endless love for you. You are not lost in a sea of people. He has pointed you out of the crowd and hand-selected you to be His very own. He knows your current situation. He knows exactly where you are, where you've been, and what you have done, yet He loves you just the same. Nothing you have done or will ever do has the power to make Him stop loving you. Bank your life upon this: He loves you and there ain't nothing you can do about it!

While Paul and Silas were in prison, at midnight they prayed and sang praises to God. At the darkest moment of their lives, they thanked God at the top of their lungs and suddenly there was an earthquake. At once, every chain was broken and every door was opened. Freedom was the result of their praise, but not just freedom for them. Freedom even came to the prison keeper and his entire household! God so powerfully transformed that dark moment into glory, He even used Paul and Silas to reach those who were once against them. Chains fall off when you give God thanks. Doors for your dreams to come to pass are opened when you give shouts of praise. Your freedom will lead to the freedom of those around you, as prison doors open and chains of bondage break everywhere that you go.

There is great power in believing and giving thanks. Get happy about what God has planned and is doing in your life. Your thanksgiving will fuel your believing, which will empower you not to faint. The joy of the Lord is your strength. Believing that you will see the goodness of the Lord in your life will strengthen you to keep putting one foot in front of the other.

The more you give thanks, the more your heart will see a picture of what God is working out in your life. When your heart sees a preview of what is just ahead, you won't give what is behind a second thought. Just dare to believe that this is not the end! What once brought you torment will now be exchanged for joy. What once caused you to cry in despair will now lead you to remember how God brought you out and actually turned that moment around to mark a fresh start in your life.

Put off that spirit of heaviness by putting on the garment of praise. Shake off depression by choosing to rejoice over the goodness of God. Refuse to attend that pity party by opening up your mouth when you least feel like it and telling your soul to bless the Lord. We will live free when we finally realize that we can tell our soul what it is allowed to focus on.

Now

Second Corinthians 2:14 says, "Now thanks be unto God, which always causeth us to triumph in Christ" (KJV). Did you notice that little, yet powerful word, *now*? Right now, right smack dab in the middle of that discouragement and pain, go ahead and begin to give God thanks. Before you see it or feel it, thank Him for the victory that already belongs to you because He always causes you to triumph! Always means always — in *all* ways. In every way, in every area of your life, and in every time, if you will trust your Father, He will always cause you to win and come out of that thing without even the smell of smoke on you!

What does it mean to be "more than a conqueror"? It means that not only do you make it out, not only do you win, but you come alive with new life! You flourish and thrive in the future that God has for you. Your heart takes flight with the dreams of what God is going to do in your life.

In Psalm 27:13, David said, "I (would have) fainted, unless I had believed to see the goodness of the LORD in the land of the living" (KJV). His statement reveals a vital key to how to make it through. If we are not going to grow weak and discouraged by the situations that are trying to overwhelm us, we have to get our eyes on something greater. The secret to us making it to the other side is in our believing. If we are bold enough to trust that our Father is going to turn this mess around and work it out for our good, we can go ahead and give God thanks right now!

There is great joy in believing and giving thanks. Get happy about what God has planned and is doing in your life. Your thanksgiving will fuel your believing, which will empower you not to faint. The joy of the Lord is your strength. Believing that you will see the goodness of the Lord in your life will strengthen you to keep putting one foot in front of the other.

Get your eyes off of the mess and catch a glimpse of what God has planned for you as He takes you out of the pit and redeems your life from destruction. Focus on the answer, not the chaos, by hooking up your mouth with the end! Like a mountain climber hooks into where he desires to go, anchor your soul in the One who is the end and that is where you will end up. He will carry you through as you believe, speak, and take another step.

The more you give thanks, the more your heart will see a picture of what God is working out in your life. When your heart sees a preview of what is just ahead, you won't give what is behind a second thought. Just dare to believe that this is not the end! What once brought you torment will now be exchanged for joy. What once caused you to cry in despair will now lead you to remember how God brought you out and actually turned that moment around to mark a fresh start in your life.

God said, "For your shame ye shall have double" (Isaiah 61:7 KJV). He is freely giving you a double load of goodness and everlasting joy shall be yours! He is the God of the second, tenth, fifty–fifth and eight hundredth and sixty-seventh chances because He is the Father of limitless, surpassing grace. The grace of Jesus will far surpass anything you think — anything you face — and go above any expectation. His love knows no end. God wants you to set your hopes as high as they will go, confident that He will do above and beyond anything you could hope, dream, or imagine!

Isaiah 61:10 says, "He hath clothed me with the garments of salvation, He hath covered me with the robe of righteousness, as a bridegroom decketh himself with ornaments, and as a bride adorneth herself with her jewels" (KJV). Let God wrap you up and clothe you in His love. He will clothe you with the joy of heaven. A prison cell might have the power to keep you in, but it cannot keep God out. Even with hell all around you, you can enjoy heaven on earth with a peace that this world can't give and unending freedom in your soul.

> Yea, though I walk through the valley of the shadow of death, I will fear no evil: for thou art with me; thy rod and thy staff they comfort me.
>
> Thou preparest a table before me in the presence of mine enemies: thou anointest my head with oil; my cup runneth over.
>
> Surely goodness and mercy shall follow me all the days of my life: and I will dwell in the house of the LORD for ever.
>
> **Psalm 23:4–6 KJV**

Even in the presence of your enemies or in the valley of the shadow of death, when your past is chasing you down and the odds are against you, you can still feast and enjoy the good life God has prepared for you. You and God are the majority! God is for you and what He is working out in your life is far greater than anything that you have gone through. Your fresh start begins right now. Before it looks like it or feels like it, thank Him right now that He has restored your soul and redeemed your life from destruction. He inhabits the praises of His people. Through the length of your days, let His presence be your dwelling place. No matter what crisis may surround you, your soul can flourish in Jesus. That jail cell may be your physical address, but there is a place within you where no one or no thing can take your freedom because you are more than a conqueror. Life doesn't have to be perfect on the outside in order for you to be happy and fulfilled on the inside. You can enjoy the freedom of a soul restored right now.

Too Much Baggage

With as much as I've traveled, you would think I would have learned the art of packing light. Unfortunately, that is not a skill I have mastered yet. It never ceases to amaze me how much I end up bringing, even on just a one-night sleepover! I always use every available bit of space in my suitcase, and I cram as many pairs of shoes and headbands as I can into an expandable backpack with my laptop, camera, and books. I also never board an airplane without a big bag of healthy goodies. (Here's a travel secret I'll throw in for free — most airlines allow an extra disposable bag when you let them know it is "food for consumption.") I realize that I am a chronic overpacker, yet I still have faith that one day I will learn better.

But for now, please take a moment to put yourself in my shoes and imagine the difficulty of navigating your way through a crowded airport terminal lugged down with unnecessary baggage. In the same way, when our souls are overburdened by the baggage of our past, we cannot move forward with the freedom and ease that Jesus intended for us to have. Holding on to weights from our past will slow us down.

Simply put, soul ties are formed when our souls are tied or emotionally connected to people, things, places, or memories. Soul ties can be healthy. For instance, when a newborn child bonds to her mother, that is a healthy soul tie. But soul ties can also be unhealthy. When we seem to be in the same place mentally year after year, unable to move beyond a hurt or toxic relationship, that is an destructive soul tie. If we were trying to run a race while chained to a pile of bricks, how could we possibly expect to cross the finish line? I've heard of an old tribe in Asia that curses its enemies by declaring, "May you remain in the same place forever." Just think about it, out of everything they could have said, that is the worst curse they could think of.

It is tormenting to live in the same place year after year, while life moves on all around you. However, that is the reality for thousands of people who give their souls permission to dwell in the past. God's plan is for you to move forward in freedom and victory, with nothing holding you back. He wants life and peace to flood your soul, not pain from your past.

He said in Joel 2:25, "I will restore to you the years that the locust hath eaten" (KJV). In other words, He will make up for the years. Quit looking at the time you feel like you have wasted — it is not too late for you! God can do a whole lot in little bit of time. He not only knows where we have been, but He knows where we are going! He knows that your best days are ahead. You have never been as happy as you are about to be. Go ahead and put a big smile on your face and declare that right now by faith!

Let this good news take root in your heart: What lies behind you cannot even come close to what's ahead of you! There is nothing behind you worth going back to. God has some wonderful surprises waiting for you that are going to thrill your heart. He knows you like no one else does and has planned the most heart-satisfying, fulfilling adventure of a life for you. As we follow God and move forward with His plan for us, we can trust that every desire of our heart will be fulfilled. Let me encourage you. Rather than postponing your joy until you obtain whatever the "next thing" is, simply allow your heart to become enthralled in His fresh love for you. Live satisfied today on your way to where you are going. Jesus is your freedom from your past, your peace in the present, and your hope for the future. He will restore your soul and comfort you like no one else can.

Time Isn't the Healer

With everything I have gone through, I can't tell you how often I have heard, "Just hang in there, it will all get better with time." However, I've come to realize that a lot of time can pass with things still no better than they were. How often are people stuck in the same place mentally, with their souls tied to the experiences and people from their past, even after months or years have come and gone? Allow me to make it clear: The passing of time will not bring you full soul freedom. Time is not the healer of all things. Only Jesus is! Only Jesus can make you whole from the inside out.

My friend, there is also no person, opportunity, or goal that can complete you; only Jesus can. Without meaning to, we can rush into things and throw ourselves into distractions that actually only serve only as a Band-Aid to cover up the wound we may not want to face. Yet, that is only temporary relief. It takes courage to finally be honest with yourself and admit when things are not ok. We cannot hide our pain behind a new relationship, work, or school. Can the right relationships or jobs bring happiness? Or course! That is something they are designed to do.

However, a soul that is whole is content even before those things take place.

We can be happy now on the way to where we are headed because we are not constantly on the hunt for the next new thing to fill the void in our souls. We are made complete and full in Jesus. God does not use distractions to merely cover up a wound. No, He is so much bigger than that!

God wants to heal you from the inside out as He fills you up to overflowing with His love. Trust me, you will know the difference between soul freedom and soul distractions. Some people make the mistake of dreaming as a way to distract themselves, to escape dealing with things. God wants you to dream. He is the most wild, fearless dreamer there is. However, He wants your pursuit of those dreams and passions to be sustained as they are birthed out of the pursuit of Him. As you make knowing Jesus the determined purpose of your life, that wonderful journey will lead you right into the fulfillment of your dreams. Remember, He can be trusted to even fulfill those secret petitions of your heart. Trust Him and follow Him freely – Father knows best!

You do not have to be stuck in the same place at this time next year. Jesus is all about the new thing He wants to do in your life now. You do not have to go one more day living in the past because there is no life back there. Any thought and tie that did not originate in Jesus are tools from the thief, designed to steal from your quality of life. Unhealthy soul ties breed darkness and depression. However, whom the Son has set free is free indeed! Jesus came to heal the broken-hearted. Because God is the Author of time, He is not confined to its limits. He can do a whole lot in a little bit of time and restore your heart in new ways at this very moment! No matter what has changed in your life, you can move forward! Step by step, you can walk out His plan of restoration. God desires to saturate your soul with His fresh, living water, to make you whole from the inside out. Your Father has unparalleled ways to refresh your life. When He restores, He makes you completely new!

CHAPTER 13

TAKE THE NEXT STEP!

R ight after the Israelites escaped Egypt, an entire army of outraged Egyptians chased them down, eager to drag them back into the same captivity from which God had just set them free. In case that wasn't bad enough, the Red Sea stood directly in front of them, blocking their way out. Yet God was not fazed. He had a plan no one else could have thought of. He knew exactly how to lead them forward into the new thing He had planned for them:

> The Egyptians pursued them, all the horses and chariots of Pharaoh and his horsemen and his army, and overtook them encamped at the [Red] Sea. . . . When Pharaoh drew near, the Israelites looked up, and behold, the Egyptians were marching after them; and the Israelites were exceedingly frightened and cried out to the Lord. And they said to Moses, Is it because there are no graves in Egypt that you have taken us away to die in the wilderness? Why have you treated us

this way and brought us out of Egypt? Did we not tell you in Egypt, Let us alone; let us serve the Egyptians? For it would have been better for us to serve the Egyptians than to die in the wilderness.

Exodus 14:9–12

Wow, talk about being stuck between a rock and a hard place! I can't begin to imagine how overwhelming that must have been for the Israelites. In their moment of crisis, their past appeared to be better than their present. When we feel pressed, our memories can also become distorted. It's easy to romanticize things that are behind us and have a false perspective of our past. Present challenges will lie to us, tell us we are not going to make it, and that life was better the way it was before.

The moment you begin to take ground and move forward, the devil will try to distract you because he knows you are standing right on the brink of your victory. Satan will try night and day to convince you that this is the end. Just like he did with the Israelites, he will attempt to make you feel stuck and overwhelmed with regret. In frustration, the Israelites blurted out, "It would have been better for us to be slaves than to die in the wilderness!" However, God never said anything about them dying out there in the wilderness. That was not the end. He had a way of escape already prepared before the problem ever arose. Yet fear blinded them from seeing the hope of a better future.

The devil will whisper in your ear, "You should just give up. It's not even worth trying. Life will never get better — life was better back then. Nothing is changing. Nothing is working." However, the moment we step out of the limitations of what we see and feel in the natural, we step into the unlimited realm of faith where nothing is impossible.

It's Not Over

God never promised us that moving forward would be easy. Challenges are sure to come. Do you want to know why? That's simple. The devil does not want you to move forward. He is afraid of your future. He can't stand to see you living the victorious life of freedom. However, you can laugh right in the face of destruction, and tell the devil he came too late to convince you that you're not going to make it. Go ahead and cheer up because victory already belongs to you!

Jesus said, "I have told you these things, so that in Me you may have [perfect] peace and confidence. In the world you have tribulation and trials and distress and frustration; but be of good cheer [take courage; be confident, certain, undaunted]! For I have overcome the world. [I have deprived it of power to harm you and have conquered it for you]" (John 16:33). Take courage! Be confident, certain, and undaunted! Whatever you may be facing today, know that this is not the end.

Remember, the devil is a liar. He would not bother telling you that you are never going to make it if your progress wasn't making him antsy. Be reinforced with fresh strength each day. Be strong in the Lord and in the power of His might and keep looking ahead. The Bible says, "Many are the afflictions of the righteous, but the LORD delivers him out of them all" (Psalm 34:19 NKJV). There is nothing too hard for God. There is no soul torment or bondage that He cannot completely set you free from. Even if you fall seven times, you shall arise! Your God will uphold you and deliver you!

There the Israelites were, panicking and feeling trapped. It did not look like they were going to make it. Of course, they could not have gone back. The Egyptians were more than ready to destroy them. But could they move forward? There was a huge sea glaring them straight in the eye, tormenting them with the promise of defeat.

Sometimes it is easy to feel like that. We look back and see all the negative experiences of our past chasing us, tightening their grip around us, pulling us back into bondage. Our past tries to make us slaves to our failures, painful memories, and the words others have spoken. We do not want to be overcome by those things. We do not want to be prisoners of our past, held captive by unhealthy soul ties. Nevertheless, sometimes moving ahead seems impossible. Fear and regret paralyze us. Shame keeps us stuck. Uncertainty consumes us as we don't know what step to take or how to move forward. Often we are left feeling overwhelmed with a sea of impossibilities standing between where we are and where we long to be.

Yet when the pressure feels the greatest and hopelessness abounds, obeying God's words changes everything. When it looked like there was no way out for the Israelites, God's words pierced through the darkness, brought peace, and revealed the way of escape. In Exodus 14:13–14 we read, "Moses told the people, Fear not; stand still (firm, confident, undismayed) and see the salvation of the Lord which He will work for you today. For the Egyptians you have seen today you shall never see again. The Lord will fight for you, and you shall hold your peace and remain at rest."

You don't have to struggle to make things work out for you. You don't have to struggle to live free from the bondage of your past. Just stand firm in trust. Stand firm in believing. Take the pressure off to perform and see that you are already free in Jesus. Do not be moved by what you see. Do not allow negative thoughts and feelings to control you. Quit trying to figure out how it is all going to work out and realize that God has already worked out your future. All we have to do is trust and obey.

We are not our own saviors. Thank God, because we would make lousy deliverers! We just aren't big enough to rescue ourselves, so we might as well quit trying. A life of trusting God is a lot more fun! Quit the struggle and enter into the rest of believing. You are simply the believer — God is the performer!

Agree with God that He has already set you free. He has already taken you out of the control of darkness, opened up the prison door, and given you all of the freedom you will ever need. Just turn on the light of the Word of God and see what is already there. Those who believe do enter into rest. Doubt strives, worries, and struggles, but faith is at rest. Faith gives thanks and rejoices. Rest and rejoice in the confidence of knowing that your Great Deliverer has a way for you that hasn't even crossed your mind and a future that is better than anything you could imagine!

Just trust. Rest and let Him restore you. There is no need to struggle to heal or fix yourself; Jesus is the only way to true healing and wholeness. Satan will try to wedge his way in, tempting you into works of the flesh. He wants you to live under the weight of striving as you work to free yourself from the past. If you are like me and have ever felt like you are taking five steps forward and then ten steps back, trying with all of your might to pedal but getting nowhere, then dear friend, it is time to jump off of that stationary bike. Leave that disappointing gerbil wheel of the works of the flesh and just be done with trying to move forward in your own strength.

The devil will try to get you busy mentally, drained emotionally, and depleted of all hope as you struggle to "fix" yourself. He wants you exhausted to the point that you just give up believing that a better life exists, choosing to hide your pain behind a smile while you are bleeding internally. Satan wants to deceive you into thinking, "As long as other people think I'm happy and that I've got my life together, I'm good." There is a life that is so much better than that! There is a restoration that is real and a freedom that belongs to you. Fear not. Jump off the gerbil wheel. Don't settle for an Instagram profile that makes it look like your life is all together while you actually live in the past, lonely, broken-hearted, and drowning in regret. Don't be deceived into believing that you will never be happy again. Stand still and see the salvation of the Lord which He will work for you today.

Jesus is the Perfect Healer. There is no emotional wound that His love cannot completely restore and make whole. There is no brokenness that can outweigh His wholeness. I promise you, His newness is far greater and more powerful than your past. Yet, the only way to receive His complete restoration is through rest. Rest and restoration. Allow those two words to ring in your spirit and become your reality. I know it sounds backwards to the world, but we rest to receive what Jesus has already done for us. If we are busy with our own useless efforts, we will never be still enough to see what God has already prepared. Satan's distractions will leave you drained, empty, and in emotional chaos. God's way will keep you emotionally strong and stable, with your soul anchored in Him.

God told Moses, "The Egyptians you have seen today you shall never see again." The same is true for you! Quit viewing your life as a hopeless, never-ending cycle of regret. You don't have to go on living with that same soul torment the devil has used to drag you down for years. Jesus changes everything. Remain at rest. The Lord will fight for you. Rest and receive real restoration. God will restore your soul and lead you in paths of righteousness, as goodness and mercy follow you all the days of your life. God's Word is like rain in your life. Let it refresh and strengthen you today. Let your soul be nourished as you drink of this living water. You will no longer be termed "forsaken" or "desolate," for the Lord delights in you! He said, "Again I will build you and you will be built" (Jeremiah 31:4). If you stand firm in His life-giving truth and water your life with His word,

God will bring change, restoration, and new life to you. He will revitalize your soul and cause you to flourish and thrive with an inner strength and resiliency.

Go Forward

Give no place to the devil. Dare to believe that a life completely free from your past exists. Do not just let go of some of the pain of your past. Let it all go! Allow no more painful memories to torment your soul or condemnation to chase after you; the Egyptians you have seen today you will never see again! Shake off the dust and the shame of yesterday. Let God's grace replace all regret. His mercies are new every single day. Quit thinking life will never be as good as it once was. If you continue to trust God, things will be better than they have ever been and you will live each day with a joy that you didn't know was possible!

Exodus 14:15-16 says, "The Lord said to Moses, Why do you cry to Me? Tell the people of Israel to go forward! Lift up your rod and stretch out your hand over the sea and divide it, and the Israelites shall go on dry ground through the midst of the sea." As they faced the Red Sea, the question every Israelite had on his or her minds was, "What do we do now?" When things get harder than you ever imagined, when you wind up in places you never would have envisioned, when you feel stuck and you simply do not know where to go — obey the wisdom of God and "GO FORWARD!" No matter where you are in life today, put one foot in front of the other and move ahead. Just like the Israelites, you will see the miraculous take place in your life when you obey God and move forward!

One of my favorite parts of the Israelites' story is that the miracle did not happen until they took the next step. I am sure the Israelites were wondering, "Wait, hold up — doesn't God see that giant sea?" I am certain that fear tightened its grip around them and they were tempted to give up, but they took the next step and God came through in a big way. In your life, He can split any blockade wide open, make a way where there seems to be no way, and cause you to walk out upon what once looked impossible.

As the Egyptians caught up with the Israelites, God wasn't up in heaven getting antsy. He knew exactly what He was going to do. He knew exactly how He was going to turn the tide in that situation. God was just waiting for His people to take the next step. The moment they took the next step and went forward, fear was eradicated and the Red Sea was split. It is the same way in our lives. When we obey what God has spoken to our hearts, take the next step, and go forward, the miraculous is unleashed.

Maybe for you, that next step means that tomorrow, you're not going to yield to depression. When depression comes knocking on your door, instead of allowing negative feelings to control you, you will choose joy and speak out, "The joy of the Lord is my strength," and "Greater is He who lives in me!" Perhaps that next step for you looks like applying for that job you didn't think you were good enough for or reaching towards that dream that is on the inside of you. Just take the step. Whatever that looks like in your situation, God is saying, "Go forward!"

At a wedding in Cana, Jesus' mother, Mary, revealed the unfailing key to miracles. She told the servants, "Whatever He says to you, do it" and water was turned into wine (John 2:1–11). Whatever He says to you, do it and those ashes in your life will be turned into something more beautiful than you could imagine. He will cause dead things to come to life and years to be restored.

This is not the time to grow weary or look back. This is your time to leave the past in the past; the miracles you have been longing for are just waiting on you to take the next step. When

God says to move forward, you don't have to know how it will all work out. Just take the step and know that He will do the rest. It is that simple. Just do it. Go forward. Be faithful to do your part and get ready to see God do the miraculous.

Wipe Out

The Israelites stepped in faith and walked across dry land. The Egyptians tried to pursue Israel, but it didn't work out for them. They tried to keep on chasing and tormenting God's children, yet they drowned in their attempts. Just like the Red Sea engulfed those Egyptians, the blood of Jesus can completely wipe out your past and your shame. Let this ring in your heart: The Egyptians you see today you will never see again. The shame of your past that the devil has used to torment you for years, you will never see again. That unforgiveness Satan has tried to keep you bound with, you will never see again. Condemnation is no match for the blood of Jesus. Leave the past in the past. There is no life behind you.

The precious blood of Jesus is more powerful than the pain you have gone through. Hebrews 9:14 says, "How much more surely shall the blood of Christ...purify our consciences from dead works?" God will always cause you to overcome by the blood of the lamb and the word of your testimony. Say what God says about you, agree with what the blood has provided, and walk in the freedom that belongs to you. Let the blood of Jesus do its full work in your life, cleansing your memory from the deadness and darkness of your past. You can live completely free from all damaging soul ties. Your mind can be a place of freedom, not pain or bondage. Don't live another day with death festering in your soul. Keep your mind stayed on Jesus and enjoy life and peace. It is time to go forward and see the salvation of the Lord. Don't let what Jesus has won be in vain in your life.

Satan wants you to stay stuck in your shame, paralyzed as you think of every reason why you can't be used by God — that's exactly what he wanted for me. He will try night and day to convince you that you are damaged goods, that your life is forever tainted by what is behind you. Yet, I pray that God will stir and strengthen your heart the way He did mine. Quit allowing lies to dictate your life! Stop letting a liar shape your future!

Lately, I've been getting rid of a lot of old clothes. In doing so, I am actually enlarging my closet and making room for new things. When you get rid of the devil's old way of thinking, you make room for the new. Out with the old and in with the new! It's time to get rid of those old thoughts, that old, depressed identity of rejection, that old shame, because Jesus came to make all things brand new. Securing the freedom that Jesus has for us begins with our thinking. That is why the Bible says we must be transformed by the renewing of our minds. Think a new way and enjoy a new quality of life. Be refreshed and renewed with the Word of God and make room for that new thing that is breaking forth in your life.

If you want that new thing, think a new way! Open up your mouth and shut the door to the devil. Don't look at where you are, look at where you are going. Don't stay where you are, go forward. When it looks and feels like all hope is gone, against hope, believe. Keep believing, keep speaking, and keep putting one foot in front of the other. When you don't know how you are going to make it — go forward. When you don't know how God is going to work this one out — go forward. When it feels like your past is trying to pull you back — go forward. Miracles are in front of you, not behind you, so go forward. Whatever He says to you, do it. Go forward. He makes a way through the sea and a path through the mighty waters. Take the next step and He will take you all the way to the other side!

CHAPTER 14

FORWARD IN HIS FAITHFULNESS

In Isaiah 43:1, we read these words, "He Who created you, O Jacob, and He Who formed you, O Israel: Fear not, for I have redeemed you [ransomed you by paying a price instead of leaving you captives]; I have called you by your name, you are Mine." From the onset, God wants you to know Who is talking to you — the one who formed you; the one who designed every detail about you, who put together your personality, gave you your smile; the one who knew you before the foundations of the world, before you were alive on this earth. This is who is looking directly at you and saying, "Fear not. You do not have to be intimidated by your past. You don't have to be afraid of your future. You don't have to cower down to those insecurities. With love flooding from His eyes, God says, "Fear not because I have redeemed you. I have ransomed you instead of leaving you captive. You are no longer a slave to shame, the prison door has been flung open wide. I have set you free; you don't have to go on living as a prisoner one more day. I didn't leave you a victim of depression. I didn't leave you stuck in shame. I gave my Son because I had to have you."

Jesus says, "I gave My life because I didn't want to go on living without you. I saw you when I was on the cross. I shed My blood for you because I wanted you. You were worth it all. I paid the highest price to redeem you because I love you. Fear not because I have made all things new. I have set you free. I have called you by a new name. You are not your past. You are not what other people have done to you. You are not what other people have said about you. You are not your mistakes. You are not alone. You are not forgotten. You are not abandoned. You are not damaged goods. You are none of those things. You are no longer a captive. You are no longer bound by the enemy. Your name is not depressed. Your name is not ashamed. I have called you by your name: YOU ARE MINE."

The devil goes around whispering the same old lies to everyone, "You don't belong anywhere. You are not anything special. You can't do anything. Nobody really cares about you." But God is saying, "You have a brand new name and identity. You are Mine. I have called you. I have appointed you. I have gifted you and given you my Holy Spirit." It is so good to belong. It is good to know that we are His.

Isaiah 43:2 goes on to say, "When you pass through the waters, I will be with you, and through the rivers, they will not overwhelm you; when you walk through the fire, you will not be burned." Hear your Father say to you, "Fear not, I am with you. Don't be overwhelmed by the cares of this life. I am with you to deliver you and carry you all the way through. Do not be moved and do not be fazed. Nothing will overtake you. I am with you and I am greater than anything that tries to stand in your way. I will always cause you to overcome. No matter what you are facing, you will make it through!"

Isaiah 43:4 says, "Because you are precious in My sight and honored, and because I love you, I will give men in return for you and peoples in exchange for your life." It all boils down to that — for God so loved the world that He gave His only begotten Son. Because you are precious in His sight and because He loves you, He has honored you with His tender mercy and care. You have His full attention, and His arms are wide open. He has honored you today with His unchanging love. He has given you His Spirit and freed you from a life of shame. He has honored you with a beautiful plan of restoration. You are going to do everything you are called to do, no longer just existing, but living the abundant life Jesus came to give; not barely making it, but experiencing the joy of being more than a conqueror as you overcome in every way to be a blessing wherever you go!

You are a living testimony of the faithfulness of God and His power to restore. The story of your life and the love within your heart will bring others to Jesus. The devil wants you to believe that your past disqualifies you from being used by God in a significant way. Satan wants you hiding in shame because he knows what a powerful magnet for God you are when you shine with the joy of Jesus. God's gifts and His callings never change or go away. Step out of hiding and step into your purpose:

"Fear not, for I am with you . . . I, even I, am the Lord, and besides Me there is no Savior. I have declared [the future]. . . . and there is no one who can deliver out of My hand. I will work, and who can hinder or reverse it?"

Isaiah 43:5, 11–13

There is no other Savior. There is no other way to real restoration. There is no other way to real joy. Remember, you are not your deliverer. Time is not your healer. Only Jesus! Only

Jesus makes broken hearts whole! He is the only One who can restore your soul and redeem the time. Your Father has declared your future. He knows the wonderful plans He has for you and He has spoken life over you. He sings over you with joy. You have a future full of hope. This is not the end. Whatever you are going through, one thing is for sure — it is not over until there is victory.

You are safe in the palm of your Father's hand. No one can snatch you away because your Father is greater than all. Your Faithful Finisher said, "I will work, and who can hinder or reverse it?" God has worked out your future — who can stop it? Nothing that is behind you can reverse what is in front of you. No guilt and no fear has the power to stop you when you realize you are; you are His. You are washed in the blood of Jesus and you belong to Him.

Isaiah 43:16 says, "Thus says the Lord, Who makes a way through the sea and a path through the mighty waters." When it looks like there is no way, Jesus is your way. In Isaiah 43:18-19, God continues, "Do not [earnestly] remember the former things; neither consider the things of old. Behold, I am doing a new thing! Now it springs forth; do you not perceive it and know it and will you not give heed to it? I will even make a way in the wilderness and rivers in the desert." God boldly declares, "Do not remember the past!" Quit going over old history – forget it already! Quit rehashing all the mistakes you have made, living in the heaviness of shame, beating yourself down thinking, "How could I have done that? Why did I let that happen?" Our quality of life is directly related to the condition and focus of our souls. We give power to those things we continue to rehash and remember, power to create perimeters and boundaries. As we keep looking back, thinking about our past, we limit our lives to those boundaries our thoughts set up.

It has been said that your life moves in the direction of your most dominant thoughts. We will never move beyond what we are constantly thinking about. We will never fully enjoy life if we are constantly looking back and thinking about things we cannot change. The devil wants to torment your soul by bombarding you with painful memories. He knows that thoughts either have the power to *paralyze you* or *propel you*. The choice is up to you. We get to choose every day what we are going to focus on.

Don't Look Back

When God wanted to save Lot and his family from Sodom and Gomorrah. The angels brought Lot and his family out of the city, "And when they had brought them forth, they said, Escape for your life! Do not look behind you or stop anywhere in the whole valley; escape to the mountains [of Moab], lest you be consumed" (Genesis 19:17). Out of everything God could have said, He said, "Do not look back." Yet as they were leaving, Lot's wife chose to look back and the moment she did, she was para-lyzed by her past. The moment she looked back, she was turned into a pillar of salt.

Looking back never takes us back where we can actually change things. Looking back just keeps us stuck right there. It keeps us from moving forward. We cannot do anything about what is behind us, but I am so thankful that God took care of our past for us. "Therefore if any person is [ingrafted] in Christ (the Messiah) he is a new creation (a new creature altogether); the old [previous moral and spiritual condition] has passed away. Behold, the fresh and new has come" (2 Corinthians 5:17).

If Lot's wife had believed that the place God was about to bring her into was greater than where she had been, she would have let go and gone forward without hesitation. Her action of looking back proved she did not trust that God could do beyond where she had been. God wants to take that mess in your life and completely transform it by His grace. If you want to save your life, you cannot look back. When we hold on to our past, we are holding on to death. Carrying around thoughts from our past will breed darkness, death, and depression. They are weights that will keep us waiting in life. In order to save your life, with everything in you, you must run forward! Do not look back! If we want to win, we cannot be passive. Passivity is simply not an option if you want to live victoriously. We must actively refuse the devil's deception and bondage and shake off the dust from the past. Don't look behind you or stop halfway! You have come too far to give up now.

In my process of moving forward, when things felt hard and I was tempted to look back and get swallowed up in regret, out of my spirit I began to boldly declare, "There is too much ahead for me to look back now!" I have heard it said that a silent Christian is a dead Christian. The devil wants to torment your soul, taunting you with things you cannot change. However, you can rise up and boldly declare what God says about you. Your words act like a magnifying glass in that the more you talk about something, the bigger it will become in your life. Combat the temptation of looking back by declaring the new thing that God is working out in your life. Don't stop halfway. Keep your eyes locked in on the freshness that is Jesus and keep moving forward.

Just like God told the Israelites, it is time to go forward! There is no life back there. One translation of Isaiah 43:18 says to "forget about it already!" Take some advice from Disney's Queen Elsa and "Let it go!" The Bible says to be carnally minded is death, but to be spiritually minded is life and peace (Romans 8:6). If we keep thinking about what is behind us, we are choosing to live in death. If we choose to believe that our story is not over and our best days are right in front of us, we will walk in life, peace, and victory.

Slam the door of your mind shut and don't even consider the things of old. God is wanting to do something brand new. Remember, out with the old and in with the new!

Don't be like Lot's wife, paralyzed by looking back. You are alive, why live stuck in the graveyard of your past? God is propelling you into the new, but He needs you to quit holding on to the past. I promise you, where God is taking you is far better than where you have been.

Just like with the Israelites, miracles are in front of you, not behind you. Wherever you are in life right now, God's grace and His strength is upon you to help you let go of the past. This is not just a good idea or suggestion; this is the difference between life and death. Just ask Lot's wife.

If you will trust and obey Him, God can do more in this one year than what has taken place in the past five years put together. You can live in a joy and a wholeness that you didn't even know existed! When God works, who can hinder or reverse it?

Time for an Address Change

Stop letting your past limit you. If you want to enjoy that new thing that is waiting to break loose, then you need to throw away those old chains and restrictions. In other words, change won't come until you change addresses. Now I'm not talking about a physical, street address. I'm talking about the place you allow your mind to live. God has instructed us to not dwell on events from long ago because wherever we allow our minds to dwell is where we will dwell. The focus of your soul determines whether you are living in the past or living in the now.

Have you ever moved and realized you weren't receiving all of your mail because you'd failed to change your address? There was a time when I waited and waited for a particular package to arrive. Finally, I called the company that mailed me the package and found they'd sent it to my old address. I was never going to get that package, no matter how long I waited! Well, you can be waiting and waiting to receive something from God, but until you change the address of your soul, you won't receive what He's sending. Quit living in the past. I promise you, God isn't sending anything there! God has already sent newness your way, but you must live in the now to pick it up. Change your address to receive the future God has for you.

> **Enlarge the place of your tent, and let the curtains of your habitations be stretched out; spare not; lengthen your cords and strengthen your stakes, for you will spread abroad to the right hand and to the left . . . Fear not, for you shall not be ashamed; neither be confounded and depressed, for you shall not be put to shame. For you shall forget the shame of your youth . . . For your Maker is your Husband–the Lord of hosts is His name–and the Holy One of Israel is your Redeemer; the God of the whole earth He is called.**
>
> Isaiah 54:2–5

It is time to enlarge the place that you live. Go forward to where you have never been before. What used to have the power to move you does not have to shake you today. Fear not! Don't live intimidated by your past. You will not be remembered for that. As you let go of what is behind you, you are making room for enlargement.

If we never take the next step and leave the past in the past, we will never experience the joy of the new thing that God is doing. It's time to go where you have never been before! Uproot the limiting thoughts of your past and stretch out the curtains of your habitation. Lengthen your cords and strengthen your stakes. Get ready, because nothing can stop you now!

The Solid Rock

I've lived in South Florida almost my entire life and have seen firsthand the catastrophic damage a huge storm can inflict on a home not built on a solid foundation. A strong foundation makes all the difference. It is often the determining factor as to what will be left standing and what will crumble.

> **So everyone who hears these words of Mine and acts upon them [obeying them] will be like a sensible (prudent, practical, wise) man who built his house upon the rock. And the rain fell and the floods came and the winds blew and beat against that house; yet it did not fall, because it had been founded on the rock. And everyone who hears these words of Mine and does not do them will be like a stupid (foolish) man who built his house upon the sand. And the rain fell and the floods came and the winds blew and beat against that house, and it fell—and great and complete was the fall of it.**
>
> Matthew 7:24–27

As it says in Matthew 7, when you hear the words of Jesus and then act on those words, you are like the wise man who built his house upon the rock — the house of your life will not fall. You can anchor your soul deep in the One who is the strength of your life. Psalm 18:2 says, "The Lord is my Rock, my Fortress, and my Deliverer; my God, my keen and firm Strength in Whom I will trust and take refuge, my Shield, and the Horn of my salvation, my High Tower." Jesus is your refuge and safe dwelling place. When Satan attempts to knock you down, you can remain stable and fixed under the shadow of the Almighty, whose power no foe can withstand. In the midst of tormenting floods and fierce winds, your soul can remain unshaken. Storms of life will come and go, but you can joyfully proclaim, "I'm still standing!"

To build your life upon the Rock, His Word must become your firm foundation. That means before you think a certain way about yourself, look to God's opinion of who you are. Before you see yourself through the glasses of your failures, let Jesus remind you He has taken away your past and made you brand new. Rather than staying trapped in shame and regret, let Him reveal His grace and show you how His mercies are fresh every single morning. Before you act, let Jesus talk to you. Hear His words of love and freedom and then build your life upon them. Frame your relationship with yourself upon the foundation of what God says.

Leave the Sinking Sand

I remember a specific night when my soul was overloaded with Satan's constant reruns of my past. Honestly, all I felt like doing was crying and giving up. Yet, through my tears, I decided to act on the Word. I knew that the only way I could come up and out was by being bold enough to speak out what I believed.

Remember, what's in you will come out in the middle of a storm; your foundation is what makes all the difference. You must consistently fill yourself up with the Word, creating a rich reservoir in your heart. When you squeeze a full sponge, water comes out. When the pressure of life squeezes you, you want the Word to come out!

Rather than crumbling in despair, God took my words of faith and turned things around. Instead of falling apart, I was strengthened with fresh joy! I kept declaring, "I'm founded upon the Rock. I will not fall or be shaken. None of these things move me! The Greater One lives in me! He loves me and He always causes me to win!" The more I spoke, the happier and freer I got! The more I rejoiced and magnified what I believed God was doing in my life, the more stable and at rest my soul became.

Simply hearing that you are loved by God but not acting upon His words by receiving His love and loving yourself is building your life on sinking sand. Hearing and not doing brings the same results as never hearing. As we are reminded in Matthew 7, a life built on those sinking sands will eventually come to a great and complete collapse. Wow, what a warning! Living by our feelings is a sure way to live an inconsistent, defeated life that is always on the verge of crisis. However, when we choose to live by what we believe, we give God the right to change whatever situation we may be facing. Peace will reign in the midst of the storm. A house built on the Rock will stand. The deeper our roots go, the stronger we will grow!

Satan wants to knock you down, but God will cause you to soar to new heights and live with a fresh strength. The devil doesn't stand a chance at destroying your confidence and contentment when you are anchored in the solid rock of Jesus. Sorry devil, you are just too late! When the floods of shame try to overwhelm your heart and the winds of regret begin to blow, you will not fall because you know who you are. You are loved and you love yourself. You have a value that no person or event can change and a worth that your past cannot alter.

Believe in yourself. Believe in your worth. Value who God has called you to be and your confidence will not falter as you grow stronger upon the Solid Rock.

CHAPTER 15

THEIR STORY CAN BE YOUR STORY

Esther

God took an orphan named Esther and used her to save a nation. She was abandoned. She was alone. She was intimidated. She didn't feel as though she was enough or believe that she was qualified. She wasn't born on the "right side of the tracks." However, without hesitation, God took this least likely candidate and used her to deliver an entire nation. She is not remembered as a victim or as having been abandoned to hopelessness. She is not remembered as one who drew back in fear. Through the power and favor of God, she stepped up and stepped into her destiny. She realized that she had come to the kingdom for such a time as was set before her. It didn't matter what laid behind her or how unqualified she may have felt in that moment. What mattered was that God was with her and this was her time to make a difference. Because she did not allow the pain of her past to write her future, Esther is remembered as a fearless queen and deliverer.

You, too, are not defined by what lies behind. What is behind you does not disqualify you for what is ahead. You are not abandoned and unwanted just because people may have rejected you in the past. Jesus will never leave you. The Bible says, "Even if my father and mother abandon me, the Lord will take care of me" (Psalm 27:10 GW). God is still there and He loves you.

He is the Father to the fatherless and the strength for the weary. Anchor your soul in His limitless love and find rest in the wholeness He has for you. Let your Father God be your confidence and your security. He is calling you to forget what lies behind and press forward.

Get out of the boat, it is time to venture out onto new waters. Keep your eyes on the prize. You were designed and destined for greatness. You have come to the kingdom for such a time as this. This is your moment in history to be who God called you to be, to make a difference and do your part to advance the kingdom of God. You will not be remembered as the girl who had that abortion. You will not be remembered as the woman who ended up in prison. You will not be remembered as the high school drop out. You will be remembered as the man or woman Jesus transformed and set free by His love. You will be remembered as one who radiates the love and joy of God. You will be remembered as that passionate go-getter, dreamer, encourager, nation changer, wife, husband, mother, father, or friend who walks in the power and authority of God.

People are waiting for you to let the past be the past and be who you are called to be. People need your story. They need your love. They need your attention. They need what you have. There are nations just waiting for the dreams within your heart to be unleashed and fulfilled. You have something precious and powerful to give to this world. Within you are miracles waiting to be unleashed, books waiting to be written, love waiting to be poured out, dreams waiting to be tapped into. There are nations on the inside of you, orphanages on the verge of being built, children anticipating your attention and care. This world needs what you have. Don't deprive it of your gifts just because of the false accusations and identity others try to put on you.

There is a God-given, anointed dream breathing on the inside of you that is wanting to break forth and take form. Your destiny will touch more than you can imagine. What will you be remembered for? The choice is up to you. Choose to let what is on the inside of you out, because people are waiting for your dream to come to life. It is your time to shine and be the fearless deliverer you were created to be.

Rahab

"Rahab the prostitute" is a woman whose sin was so linked to her, it was practically part of her name. However, one day everything changed. She made the bold choice not to be bound by that identity. She chose to follow God. She chose to leave her past behind and be remembered for something new.

Hebrews 11:31 says, "[Prompted] by faith Rahab the prostitute was not destroyed along with those who refused to believe and obey, because she had received the spies in peace [without enmity]." Clearly, Rahab had not lived a perfect life. She had made a lot of mistakes. Perhaps she experienced pain or rejection and never fully believed that she was accepted or loved, so she found herself trapped, trying to fill that void. Maybe she was leading a very lonely life and didn't know how to escape her low sense of self-worth. Perhaps she never felt beautiful unless she slept with a man. Whatever the cause, whatever brokenness may have led her to her actions, she was a prostitute.

What I love most about Rahab, however, is that when the opportunity presented itself, when she reached a vital crossroad in which she could have gone with what she was expected by others to do or what God called her to do, she chose correctly. She chose to not look at all of the wrong she had done. She chose to no longer live and act within the confinements of her past. She could have easily said, "I'm a prostitute. There is no way I'm good enough for God to use me." But she chose to take the fresh start that was set before her. Rahab left the past and escaped the rut of her old lifestyle. By deciding to trust God and make the choice that took courage and bravery, she saved her future. By faith, she decided to act in line, not with what she had been, but with who God had called her to be. Choosing faith over her failures saved her future. We destroy our future by staying stuck in the pain, failures, and shame of our past. Rahab could have easily identified herself by her past and her sins. She could have easily remained within the boundaries of the name others had given her. Instead, at that crossroads moment, she made the vital decision to believe God. By faith, she decided to act in line, not with what she had been, but with who God had called her to be. Choosing faith over her failures saved her future.

There is nothing in your life that God cannot turn around for your good if you will choose to believe. You are not unqualified by your past and you are not rejected because of your failures. God told Rahab that she was good enough. Not once did He think to say, "No, I don't want to use you, Rahab. You have lived a sinful life; you are not worth delivering. Surely there is someone better in Jericho to save." God was not ashamed to use her. God did not look down on her and wonder, "Surely there is someone else more proper, more talented, more beautiful, more qualified, more deserving." He did not look at her with disgust. Rather, He looked at her with compassion and saw the beauty of a believing heart that desired change. Rahab separated herself from the actions of her past and God separated her for His glory

By refusing to no longer identify herself with what she had been in the past and the name others had given her, she also rescued the future of her family. Rahab's faith impacted her own life, impacted her family, and ultimately touched every generation that walked on the face of the earth after her. She who was once considered worthless and damaged goods was given a clean slate. Her obedience led her into great honor and blessing; as she rescued her family line, she paved the way for the birth of Jesus!

Strength is required to go against the current, to leave the past behind, and to act opposite of what others expect from you. It takes courage to believe that a better life is available. Believing reveals strength and there is strength found in believing. By choosing faith, we leave our failures behind and stretch forth to what is prepared and waiting ahead of us. However, the path of those who refuse to believe that God can turn things around and give a brand new start leads to destruction. An unbelieving heart will never move beyond what it has always seen. Doubt keeps you out, but faith moves you forward. Doubt leads to destruction, but faith brings freedom. Choosing to trust that God has given you a clean slate and believing that you will see His goodness in your life gives place to a strength that will propel you into the new.

Just like Rahab's bold believing saved her future and gave her access to the scarlet chord that preserved her life, firmly believing what the blood of Jesus has done for you will deliver you out of the shame into the glorious future that God has for you. God thrives on plucking out the lonely, the damaged goods, and the so-called nobodies and setting them apart for a mighty turnaround. He takes the unwanted things of this world and marks them by His goodness and glory. He is an expert in taking the most unlikely things and transforming them into something magnificent! Like Jerry Savelle has often said, "God is a master at making champions out of nobodies!" What He has done for one, He will do for another.

Sarah

When God first told Abraham that he and Sarah were going to have a baby, Sarah laughed in unbelief. Yet she did not stay there. Hebrews 11:11 says that Sarah counted God faithful to do what He said. Her believing caused that God-given dream to become a God-given reality. Sarah went from barren to fulfilled. Unbelief did not define her life and she became the mother of many nations.

She chose to see beyond the confinements of the way life had always been and to grasp what God envisioned for her. She chose to look beyond what her natural strength and ideas could produce. Sarah counted God faithful, and her faith opened up a realm of possibilities that were previously impossible. God took her beyond the rut of what always had been and fulfilled her dream. Sarah is not remembered for her unbelief, she is remembered for taking God at His word. She is remembered as a believer who refused to back down, whose legacy of faith continues to this very day. She has affected every generation by being the mother that she was destined to be.

Just like Sarah, we can start bad and finish good! Don't get stuck in unbelief just because a promise of God has taken longer than you wanted it to. God is faithful to watch over His Word to perform it! Faithful is He who has called you and He is faithful to do it. Within you is a God-given dream. See what God sees for your life and refuse to let the passage of time or thoughts of doubt cause you to back down. No matter what God has called you to do in life, if you don't quit believing, you will live out the fulfillment of that dream. If He has called you to be a wife and mother, don't let go of that dream and God will fulfill it! Every word from God will be fulfilled; all things are possible to the one who believes! No dream is too big, nor is any dream too insignificant. You are designed for greatness and destined to impact the lives of others for the glory of God.

The Woman with the Issue of Blood

God can make the rest of your life, the best of your life! He can make you whole from the inside out and give you a fresh start that is more beautiful than anything you could have imagined. I love how clearly the story of the woman with the issue of blood illustrates that truth (Mark 5:25–34). This woman had a massive physical problem. For 12 years, she went from doctor to doctor, spending all the money she had, hoping to get better, but she kept getting worse. The problem didn't go away with time; rather, it got bigger. She wasn't able to enjoy a normal life as her issue consumed every part of who she was.

But then, the woman heard Jesus was in her town, so she pressed through the crowd. She was determined to get to Jesus. She kept saying to herself, "If I may but touch the hem of His garment, I will be made whole." The woman pressed through the huge crowd of people surrounding Jesus until, almost out of breath, she finally was close enough and she touched Him. Jesus stopped in His tracks. There were people all around Him, shoulder to shoulder, but He stopped and asked, "Who touched Me?" No doubt, numerous people were touching Him, but this was different. This was a touch of faith. Power had gone out of Him. Life had been released. The woman looked at Jesus and said, "I did it. I was the one who touched you." With eyes full of grace and tender love, He said, "Daughter, your faith has made you whole."

Jesus wants the same for you. He wants to look at you and say, "Child, your faith has made you whole."

I'm a pastor's kid. I grew up in children's church and I watched all of the Bible cartoons. Throughout the years, I heard countless sermons preached on the woman with the issue of blood. I've always enjoyed and learned from this story, but it was not until I was going through a difficult time in my own life that this passage from the Bible became a living factor to me. I remember reading the Bible in my bedroom one night and when I read this story, it was as though it was the very first time I had heard it. It finally hit me. This woman had this problem for 12 years. That's a long time! Doctors couldn't help her, and she couldn't help herself. The problem wasn't going away — it was just getting worse. She had no reason to believe that anything could change, yet she believed. Even though pain and disappointment had woven its way into the fabric of her life and she had no logical basis to think that anything could get better, but her faith was ignited the moment she heard. She heard, believed, and knew that everything would be different. Her trust in Jesus moved her to press past the hopelessness, fear, doubts, distractions, and pain. What doctors couldn't change and what she couldn't do for herself, Jesus changed in an instant. Jesus changes everything. All at once I saw it. Jesus said, "Daughter, your faith has made you whole." The woman was not just healed, she was made whole. I became convinced that if I would just bring the pieces of my life to Jesus, He would heal me. Jesus wants to heal us every place we hurt. He wants to take away the guilt, pain, and fear. He desires to redeem our lives and not just heal our hearts, but make us whole. He doesn't want us to settle for what used to be, for what has become "normal" to us, but He desires to make life better than it has ever been before. Jesus wants to make us whole from the inside, out.

For 12 years, the woman with the issue of blood did everything she knew to do, but she kept getting worse and worse. However, she touched Jesus and everything changed. She did not die in hopelessness. She refused to accept her pain as her new "norm." No matter what the impossibility, no matter how long you have dealt with something, refuse to accept that brokenness as your residence. Refuse to accept that shame as an unavoidable part of your life. Nothing is impossible with God! He loves you and He is faithful! He is turning your situation around for good. Like this woman, you will be remembered as the child whose faith made you whole.

The Widow

Second Kings 4 tells the story of a widow on the brink of losing her two sons. Her situation looked impossible. She had lost her husband, and was faced with insurmountable debt. Her sons would be forced to live their lives as slaves to the creditor. When the prophet Elisha discovered that the woman had a single jar of oil, he gave her these instructions:

> Go around and borrow vessels from all your neighbors, empty vessels—and not a few. And when you come in, shut the door upon you and your sons. Then pour out [the oil you have] into all those vessels, setting aside each one when it is full.
>
> So she went from him and shut the door upon herself and her sons, who brought to her the vessels as she poured the oil. When the vessels were all full, she said to her son, Bring me another vessel. And he said to her, There is not a one left. Then the oil stopped multiplying.
>
> Then she came and told the man of God. He said, Go, sell the oil and pay your debt, and you and your sons live on the rest.

2 Kings 4:3–7

What a remarkable story! And if you will trust God today, He will not disappoint you either. This woman started right where she was at and God met her in that place. Rather than being paralyzed by the heartbreak of her past, her steps of faith took her forward into the miraculous. God filled all brokenness with His wholeness.

I love a statement that one minister made about this story. He said, "The miracles of tomorrow happen when we shut the door on the past." When we choose to let go and forget what lies behind, we give God permission to work on our behalf to transform it for our good. When we give our past to God and choose to trust Him with our future, we will see the miraculous take place in our present. Your Father has miracles planned for today, He is just waiting for you to shut the door on yesterday, leave the past in the past, and take the next step!

Just like in the lives of all of the overcomers in the Bible, you have a guaranteed victory as long as you refuse to quit. The devil will try to get you to think that he has you just where he wants you. He will attempt to convince you that it's all over. But don't give up! Just like he didn't have the final word in the lives of Esther or the woman caught in adultery, his plan of destruction will be superseded and turned around by grace if you continue to take the next step of trust.

The New Living Translation in Acts 9:1 says, "Saul was uttering threats with every breath and was eager to kill the Lord's followers." Yet, God gave him a new name and a new life. Without shame, God made it clear "this man is a chosen instrument of Mine" (Acts 9:15 AMP). David was a murderer and an adulterer, but more importantly, he was a quick repenter. God called him, "A man after my own heart." He was not disqualified by His past. Rather, his life was a constant portrayal of the overcoming goodness of His Father God! Moses started out in fear and shame, but finally stepped out of His limited ability and stepped into the fathomless power of the Great I Am. There is no one God cannot use and no life He cannot turn around if you will dare to trust Him and follow His plan of freedom. God has a new identity for you!

He Is Still Writing Your Story

The Bible is full of ordinary people — people who made mistakes, experienced failures, and felt pain — yet mercy and grace win as these imperfect people chose to let go of their past, cling to faith, and march on towards their glorious future. God takes the ordinary things of this world and transforms them into something extraordinary and He is not finished with you yet. It's not over till it ends in victory.

This is your Father's plan for you. God wants to heal your heart, restore your soul and turn things around for your good. Expect the unexpected! If you believe, all things are possible. He will give you hope in your final outcome and give you a better life than you imagined. He has chosen you and not once has He regretted His choice! God is not afraid of what [other] people might think if He associates with you. Sure others might think that way and may abandon you because they care about what others might say, but God never will. He knew it all, yet He still sees you. He is in love with you and He is not going anywhere. He will never leave you and He will carry you all the way through.

Satan wants you to think that this regret will be forever. The truth of the matter is that the devil is so afraid of the power that is in you to overcome that he will work night and day to torment you by trying to attach things from the outside. That's what he did to me. Can I just be honest with you? Having been a people-pleaser in the past, I gave the voice of others way too much access and weight in my life. Over time, some of their negative opinions became my opinion of myself. I started seeing myself as damaged goods and forever tainted by my past. Fear tried to grip me as I began to wonder, "What can I even do now? What difference can I ever make? Who would want to listen to me now? I'm divorced. Nobody really cares about me anymore. Nobody wants anything or expects anything good from me anymore." I slowly became convinced that God could never use me again and that my life would be void of meaning. Don't get stuck there! That shame cannot last when you realize that Jesus has set you free from your past! Refuse to see yourself as damaged goods! Refuse to beat yourself down. Realize that it is all just a trap from the enemy because he is so afraid of your God-given purpose. Do not allow Satan to gain access into your soul through the vehicle of the voices of man. Be rooted in the Father's love for you and enjoy the freedom of an unwavering identity.

He will restore and strengthen the right relationships and bring new, uplifting friendships. God desires for your relationships to add to your life, not discourage and drain you of hope. I am not saying that you should isolate yourself, but I am saying that it is very important to guard who you let enter in your inner circle of influence. Protect who you spend your time with and allow to speak into your life. Relationships can either pull you up or pull you down. Trust me, the devil will try any open door that he can and he is more than ready to use the people in your life to influence you to re-hash and re-live your past. Follow your heart in your conversations with others. Be careful with what you are talking about, because our words have a magnifying and drawing power within our lives. That is why it is vital to have people within your life that will point you forward, not backwards. Trust God that He will send you friendships that will bless your life with freedom and joy and people who will be used by God to pull out the treasures and the beauty that God has placed within you, as you have the blessing of doing the same in their lives. He will surround you with people who see the good in you, even when you are struggling to see it. They will remind you what God says about your life, your future, and where you are headed.

According to The Message translation of 1 Peter 1:3 and 1 Corinthians 1:30, a fresh start and a clean slate comes from God and you have everything to live for! Now, when you look at your life and ponder your future, see it all through the eyes of grace. No longer consult your past to determine your worth. No longer measure the possibilities of your future by looking back at the limitations that were behind you. I hear God saying, "Don't go on holding to the chains that I have already loosed. Don't continue holding on to death when I have given you life. Why go on living in that old, defeated prison cell when its gates have already crumbled by My glory? I have already carried you out of that bondage of shame into freedom!"

When God delivered the three Hebrew children from the fire, they left the scene without even having the smell of smoke on them. God wants to redeem your life from destruction, heal you and make you whole to the point where you don't even have the slightest scent of the past on you. He will make you whole to the point that it will be unrecognizable that you even went through that! There are no scars, your heart doesn't hurt, and your future is not tainted by your past. The things of your past become a distant memory in the freedom of your present. No longer will you subconsciously act like a victim, but as an overcomer, you will be free to be the you that you were always meant to be.

Just like in the lives of all of the overcomers in the Bible, you have a guaranteed victory as long as you refuse to quit. The devil will try to get you to think that he has you just where he wants you. He will attempt to convince you that it's all over. But don't give up! Just like he didn't have the final word in the lives of Esther or the woman caught in adultery, his plan of destruction will be superseded and turned around by grace if you continue to take the next step of trust.

That truth has changed my life and has completely transformed the way I view myself and my future. How refreshing it is to know that God knew everything that would ever happen. Nothing is hidden to Him. When things get messy, people tend to leave the scene because they don't want to get their hands dirty. But not God. He'll pick you up right out of the middle of that mess. He is not the least bit ashamed of you. He loves you just as much as He loves Jesus and He is just as much your Father as He is to Jesus.

The fact that you are alive, breathing, and walking on this earth means that God has a victory with your name on it. You are designed for greatness. Before the foundations of the world, you were destined to be remembered for something greater than yourself. Your story is not over yet. God has a future and a hope for you. Saying that got me through many sleepless nights.

I find such comfort and strength to move forward knowing that my Father sees me and He loves me just the same and wants to use me. My mistakes are not bigger than the plan He has for me. My failures have not taken away His call. His gifts and His callings are without repentance and His love is unconditional, unchanging, and everlasting.

You've got far too much to live for to give up now. There are too many adventures ahead of you for you to live to look back now! There are too many people waiting to hear your story of God's deliverance for you to stay hiding in guilt and condemnation. Condemnation and guilt has never been able to change anybody but the love, forgiveness, grace, and empowerment of Jesus does!

God has an incredible plan for your life and that plan is not dependent upon what you've done or been though in your past. His plan is greater than your mistakes, because He is bigger than your mistakes. His plan is bigger than the storms that you may face because He is greater than the storms. What He did for those in the Bible, He will do for you. Your story is not over yet. God is not finished with you yet. Don't give up. You will not be remembered for that. You will be remembered as the person who trusted God and watched Him turn the tide in your life. You are moving forward!

CONCLUSION

What Will You Be Remembered For?

CHAPTER 16

GET HAPPY

Opposite Day

The moment it feels like you are being backed into a corner and everything around you is trying to persuade you that it's too late, that is the very moment to get happy! I am a strong believer that when we are most tempted to give up, we are actually right on the verge of our biggest breakthrough. The devil would not waste his time trying to talk you out of something that isn't working. The reason he is so persistent about trying to get you to quit moving forward by tormenting you with your past is because your impending victory is making him antsy. He is afraid of your future.

The Bible refers to the devil as "the father of lies" (John 8:44). Lies are the only language he speaks. That means when he whispers in your ear you will never make it, that life will never be the same again, that you will never live free, you can take that as further confirmation that things are about to break loose in your life and get better than they have ever been before! Let's follow the wisdom in the Book of James and count it all joy when we encounter any kind of trials or difficulties. Just rejoice in the Lord always and go ahead and keep on rejoicing, because this is not the end!

When I was little, if someone ever said something to me that I didn't like or approve of, I would just get sassy and smile saying, "Well actually, today is opposite day." On opposite day, no remark could get me down, as I chose to only believe the best. Let me reassure you that every day with the devil is opposite day. When he tries to convince you that nothing is working and nothing will change, rather than throwing your hands up and throwing it all away, just throw your hands up and give God some praise! Let every lie backfire on the enemy and propel you into praise. Rather than allowing his pestering whispers to take you on that downward cycle of discouragement, rise up in faith by giving God thanks for what He is about to do in your life. Let what used to discourage you crank up and fuel your thanksgiving! No matter what the devil tries to bring your way, this is the sure way to come up and come out on top. Remember, the enemy would not waste his time trying to get you to give up if he wasn't afraid of where you are headed. The reason the enemy works overtime to try to convince you that you are never going to make it is because of the simple fact that you are gonna make it! The devil is not big enough to stop the great plan God has for you.

That is why his major tactics are deception and distraction. Like dangling a carrot in front of a rabbit, he will try night and day to distract you with the rewind button of your past. He will use any open door to try to get you to believe his lie that you are damaged goods. He wants you to believe that you are not good enough to be used by God so you will never dare to dream that there could be more to life. The enemy doesn't have the power to stop you, but he also knows that you can stop yourself if you get stuck in your past, only seeing what was, not what could be. When we are so focused on what is behind us, we will never step into what is in front of us.

Let's take our feet off the brakes when God is wanting things to break loose in our lives! God has hit the accelerator and He is taking you forward! He will take you down smooth, clear paths if you will dare to believe that the best is yet to come. Why allow the enemy's nagging to intimidate you? He cannot overcome you if you refuse to back down. When the pressure feels the strongest, don't quit! The finish line is just around the corner. Romans 8:31 reminds us, "With God on our side like this, how can we lose?" (MSG). This is why we can laugh right in the face of destruction and famine! When everything around you looks like you're not gonna make it, go ahead and stir up your joy. How can you lose? God is on your side! Having done all to stand, just keep on standing. Victory is inevitable for those who refuse to let go of their joy. If you don't quit, you will win!

Nehemiah 8:10 says, "For the joy of the Lord is your strength and stronghold." One definition of the word *stronghold* is "fortified defense." In other words, when we refuse to allow the devil to steal our joy, regardless of contradictory circumstances, it is as though we are building an impenetrable shield of protection round about us and defeat is unable to have the final word. The wonderful part about it all is that our joy doesn't have anything to do with what we are facing. Right in the midst of chaos and destruction, we can be full of praise and joy, not because of what we see, but because of what we believe! It is our choice to rejoice. We have the power to believe that no matter what comes our way, somehow, some way God is going to work it out for our good. Satan has no defense against us when we choose joy and stand firm in our believing.

Look at the life of the apostle Paul. When he was ship-wrecked (Acts 27), he told the other passengers, "Be of good cheer!" When they were stranded on an island and a snake bit him (Acts 28), he just shook that baby off. He knew that imprisonment and afflictions were in his near future, yet he boldly declared, "None of these things move me!" He ended up in the most horrific prison of that time, trapped in sewage waist deep and he still said, "Rejoice in the Lord always, again I say rejoice" (Philippians 4:4). They told him, "We are going to kill you Paul." His response was nothing short of amazing: "Well you will actually be doing me a favor because to live is Christ and to die is gain" (Philippians 1:21).

Our joy has everything to do with our victory. God has wonderful plans for your life. He is so much bigger than the pain you have endured and if you will trust Him, He can take those very same plans that the devil meant to destroy your life and turn them around for your good. He will take you from where you are to where you are meant to be, as long as you refuse to let go of your joy.

I Believe God

Something was ignited in my heart the moment I heard Jerry Savelle say, "If the devil can't steal your joy, he can't keep your goods!" He has said, "For every negative thing that comes your way, there is something positive on the other side that is wanting to break through if you maintain the right attitude." Our attitude has everything to do with our outcome!

In the Book of Genesis, Joseph was given a dream, but it didn't look like it would ever come to pass. His brothers sold him into slavery. He was wrongfully accused and imprisoned. Joseph could have easily given up and stopped believing in his dream.

In my opinion, if anyone has ever had a right to live the remainder of his life feeling sorry for himself over the things done to him that he did not deserve, it would be Joseph. However, Joseph's life is proof that pity parties will never take us out of the pit and into the palace. Joseph kept his attitude and expectancy up, and God kept picking him up and setting him on high.

Our belief in God is the very thing that enables Him to do the impossible. Joseph said, "You planned evil against me, but God used those same plans for my good" (Genesis 50:20 MSG). Time and time again, God can take the very same plans the enemy intended to destroy your life and turn them around by His grace into something that is more beautiful than you could ever imagine and cause it to actually end up working out for your good. How He can do that every single time, I have no idea, but you don't get to be God unless you can do things like that! You can choose to go forward and say these three simple words, "*I believe God.*"

God will blindside the enemy each and every time. The enemy will hope that divorce will leave you hiding in shame, that your time in prison will rob you of your sense of value and purpose. He desires nothing more than for you to find your identity in the mistakes you have made and to let your past define who you are. The devil wants to torment your mind with your past, hoping to keep you stuck in the things you cannot change. However, no matter where life may find you today, at this very moment the choice is up to you. You can choose to allow the devil to have the final say in your life. You can throw up your hands, give up on your dreams, give up on your life, continuing to merely exist, broken on the inside, stuck in the past. Or you can choose to go forward and say these three simple words, "I BELIEVE GOD."

Don't let anything your adversary does intimidate you. Like Brother Jerry Savelle says, "Just keep the devil guessing." He'll think that he has you right where he wants you. Right after the enemy fires his best shot, he will think there is no way you will get back up. Well, just rise up with a smile, dust yourself off, and ask, "Is that all you've got!?" Get back up and keep on going.

Keep believing God and blindsiding the devil. The Bible reassures us that we have that same spirit of faith, the spirit of an overcomer. Like Paul, we can declare, "But none of those things move me! That matters little! I am going to finish my course with joy!"

I'm telling you, the devil cannot defeat you! Nothing can keep you down! When you rejoice, not based on what you see but based on what you believe, your victory is guaranteed. You cannot lose if you refuse to quit. Just get bold in your God because you know that the best is before you. Let the truth of God's Word build a sturdy and steady boldness within you that you can't get from anywhere else. There is an unshakeable confidence built into the fabric of your being when you *know* something.

> "And I am *convinced and sure* of this very thing, that He Who began a good work in you will continue until the day of Jesus Christ [right up to the time of His return], developing [that good work] and perfecting and bringing it to full completion in you."

> Philippians 1:6

> "We are *assured and know* that [God being a partner in their labor] all things work together and are [fitting into a plan] for good to and for those who love God and are called according to [His] design and purpose."

> Romans 8:28

"For I am *well assured and indeed know* that…this will turn out for my preservation (for the spiritual health and welfare of my own soul)."

Philippians 1:19

As the saying goes, "Come hell or high water," you can stand firm in your place of believing because you already know how this thing is going to turn out. The devil loves the pile-on effect. He will come from all angles, trying tirelessly to back you into a corner and convince you nothing is working, that nothing is changing. However, you can rest assured, fully convinced that your God is greater, and He is on your side.

When Jairus was at the lowest point of his life, when it looked like it was too late for his daughter's life to be saved, Jesus revealed the secret to seeing the impossible take place right before his eyes (Luke 8:49–56). Immediately after Jairus was told that his daughter had died, Jesus spoke these simple, yet powerful words to him, "Fear not, only believe." What a powerful statement! Fear is the opposite of faith; it is a result of doubt. Fear says, "It will never change. God can't use me. I will never make it." Yet, faith expects God to turn things around. Faith says, "Nothing is impossible!"

Throughout the gospels, Jesus said time and time again, let it be done "according to your faith." It is clear that our believing dictates what Jesus can do in our lives. God can do anything, but He only has a right to do for you what you believe that He can do. Just like Jesus raised up Jairus' daughter, He can take what looks like the end and transform it into your fresh start. There are no impossibilities and no need to be intimidated by your past. Fear not, only believe!

Lazarus had been in the tomb for over four days (John 11). It looked like it was too late, yet Jesus said, "If you believe, you will see the glory of God." One definition of the glory of God is the goodness of God. If you believe, you will see the goodness of God in your life. There is nothing that has gone too far that Jesus cannot redeem and make it brand new. God just needs you to give Him something to work with. Regardless of what circumstances may be shouting to you, believe that you will see God's goodness in your life because when you keep believing, you will see it. In other words, see it on the inside and you will see it on the outside. There is nothing to fear because nothing is impossible.

Promised Completion

It is never too late with God. He is bigger than our past and greater than time. However, it is our believing that makes all the difference and secures the victory that belongs to us. Believing is what causes dead things to come to life and allows God to turn ashes into beauty. Jerry Savelle has said, "Dreams come true for those who stay true to their dreams." Our belief in God will take us from where we are to where we want to be. Believing opens the door for God to heal our hearts, restore our souls, and do a new thing in our lives.

Hebrews 10:35 says, "Cast not away therefore your confidence, which hath great recompense of reward" (KJV). The Amplified version puts it this way, "Do not, therefore, fling away your fearless confidence, for it carries a great and glorious compensation of reward." The Message version says, "So don't throw it all away now. You were sure of yourselves then. It's still a sure thing! But you need to stick it out, staying with God's plan so you'll be there for the promised completion." All of these versions are telling us that we have to give God something to work with.

You do the believing, God will do the performing. As simple as that may sound, sometimes we tend to mix it up. We try to change ourselves, heal our wounded souls, and let go of our past in our own strength. However, we cannot fix ourselves. Only our Savior Jesus can do that! Jesus is the only One who can save our sinking souls and redeem our lives from destruction. We do the believing, He does the performing. We do the believing, He does the healing and restoring. We do the believing, He does the changing, the rearranging, and the turning of those things in our lives!

Hebrews reveals to us that those who believe have entered into rest (Hebrews 4:3). When we truly believe God to do a powerful work in our souls, we are at rest. We quit trying to do it on our own. We do not have to struggle to produce; we just need to rest, lean, and rely a little bit more on our Father God.

Sometimes when people think about faith and believing God, they picture someone who is worried, anxious, tired, and running out of strength as they work to believe God. But that is not what it looks like to believe God. True believing carries real joy with it. The pressure is not on you to perform, rather, all the expectation is directed towards God. From a place of rest, speak out what God says about your situation. Fear not, only believe. Like relaxing in a comfy, oversized chair, when you are in a position of rest, you are not trying to hold yourself up. You fully allow yourself to be supported. Let go and rest in God. Let go of the weight of worry and sink into marvelous comfort. Stay in that place of restful, confident, joyful believing because He is faithful to complete what He has started in your life. You are right on the verge of your biggest breakthrough! Just stick it out. Stay with God's plan and you will make it to your promised completion!

CHAPTER 17

KEEP GOING

When I ran cross country, bolting out after hearing the whistle blow at the start of a race was always exciting. And nothing compared to the thrill of crossing the finish line because it meant I'd made it, that all my hard work finally paid off. However, in the middle of that race, discouragement had the chance to set in. In the middle portion of the race, it was easy to lose focus and get my attention off of finishing and on to how I didn't feel like I had the strength to go on.

I often think of the time when Jesus and His disciples loaded into a boat and Jesus said, "Let us go over to the other side" (Mark 4:35–41). Off they went. Everything was going according to plan when out of nowhere, a huge storm of hurricane proportions appeared. But in the middle of the lake, with the winds blowing and the waves violently beating against the boat, the disciples became despondent.

I heard someone say, "Everything looks like a failure when you are in the middle of it." It's exciting to have big dreams and ambitions. Inspiration and good intentions make it relatively easy to start off with an optimistic heart. And who doesn't love crossing the finish line? But it's in the middle when we can lose hope and focus.

Maybe that is where you are right now. Maybe you are in the middle of the process of moving forward. Maybe an uplifting conversation or something you read in the Bible really encouraged you to take a step. You finally mustered up the courage to leave that abusive relationship, or perhaps you finally made the decision of faith to forgive yourself and others.

You finally started down the path of a life of freedom, and things had been going good — you felt lighter and happier and were making progress — but then a storm came and things have gotten harder. You realized that soul ties are still there. Feelings are still there. Pain is still there. Memories are still there and they still hurt. Tragedy happens. You feel alone. You feel discouraged. You don't see a way to make it through.

That's what happened to the disciples in the middle of their journey when the storm came. At their wits end, they ran to Jesus and found Him asleep in the back of the boat. Terrified, they woke Him up and said, "Don't You even care about us!?"

But Jesus got up and rebuked the winds and the waves and all at once, there was a great calm. Jesus spoke and changed everything. Where there once was chaos, there was tangible peace. I heard one minister, Jerry Savelle say, "At the other side of every great storm, there is a great victory. On the other side of every mega storm, there is a mega calm."

Jesus turned to His disciples and asked, "Where is your faith?" That's a great question to ask yourself when you are stuck in the middle. Where is your faith? Is your faith in the failures of your past or is it in the precious blood of Jesus? Is your faith in what was or in what God is doing to turn it all around for your good? Where is your faith?

You Are Going to the Other Side

When I was smack dab in the middle of what was by far the darkest and hardest time of my life, God gave me a picture of myself. During a time when I felt so lost and alone, had no idea where my life was going, when I did not feel beautiful in any way, and when I least expected it – God showed me how He sees me. In my heart, He showed me a picture in which I was wearing a beautiful, flowing, white dress with flowers cascading from my hair. I was dancing without a care in the world. With my arms wide open, there I was spinning in a forest with the biggest, most radiant smile on my face, just laughing with Jesus. I was beaming with life and joy. The beauty and fullness of Jesus radiated from the very core of who I was.

With that picture, God spoke to my heart and I knew without a doubt that I would be happy again. It was then that I knew the pain wasn't going to last forever. He was making all things new. It was a "let us go to the other side" moment for me. That image was something I would continually hold on to. When the storms raged and discouragement tried to overpower me, I would close my eyes and see that picture. God wants you to see yourself the way He sees you.

Jeremiah 31:3 says: "The Lord appeared from of old to me . . . saying, Yes, I have loved you with an everlasting love; therefore with loving-kindness have I drawn you and continued My faithfulness to you." The Message puts it this way, "I've never quit loving you and never will. Expect love, love and more love!" Your Father God has never quit loving you and He never will! He loves you, He cares about you, and He is saying directly to you, "Let us go to the other side." You can trust Him and depend on Him. Because God is FOR you, you can move FORWARD!

For some reason, verse 3 of Jeremiah 31 used to be the only verse in that chapter I read. But one night I kept on reading, and I'm so happy I did! God goes on to say, "Again I will build you and you will be built, O Virgin Israel! You will again be adorned with your timbrels [small one-headed drums] and go forth in the dancing [chorus] of those who make merry. Again you shall plant vineyards upon the mountains of Samaria; the planters shall plant and make the fruit common and enjoy it [undisturbed] . . . Sing aloud with gladness for Jacob, and shout for the head of the nations [on account of the chosen people, Israel]. Proclaim, praise, and say, The Lord has saved His people! . . . For the Lord has ransomed Jacob and has redeemed him from the hand of him who was too strong for him" (Jeremiah 31:4–5, 7, 11).

As the chapter continues, God beautifully paints a picture of restoration founded on His unchanging and unfailing love. He wants to rebuild things in your life for you to go forth and make merry! God has plans for your life to be fruitful and satisfying!

> They shall come and sing aloud on the height of Zion and shall flow together and be radiant with joy over the goodness of the Lord...And their life shall be like a watered garden and they shall not sorrow or languish any more at all. Then will the maidens rejoice in the dance, and the young men and old together. For I will turn their mourning into joy and will comfort them and make them rejoice after their sorrow. I will satisfy fully the life of the priests with abundance and my people will be satisfied with my goodness, says the Lord.
>
> vv. 12–14

Wow, I love that! God wants to take you to the height of Zion. That's like Him saying, "Don't be ashamed of your past.

Don't hold your head down low. Don't be intimidated by people and by what they may think of you. Arise and shine! I've raised you up out of that. I've lifted you out of that shame. I've taken you out of that brokenness. I have redeemed you from that which was too strong for you. I've redeemed your life from destruction."

Be radiant with joy over the goodness of the Lord. Get your focus on Jesus and the unfailing goodness of God in your life. Your life shall be like a well-watered garden — no longer dead and dry, but vibrant and alive. You'll be fresh and new; restored and refreshed. His restoration is so powerful that you shall not sorrow any more at all!

The King James Version of verse 13 uses the word "virgin" in place of the word "maidens," "Then shall the virgin rejoice and dance." I love how God inspired the use of the word "virgin" and said she will rejoice in the dance. I believe that virgin is specifically used because God wants you to know that is how He sees you and He wants you to see yourself that way. All because of what Jesus has done by shedding His precious blood for you, God sees you as innocent. You are clean and washed white as snow. When God looks at you, He doesn't see everything you have done wrong. He sees you — the real you, whole and complete in Jesus.

I dare you to live while you are alive. You might as well be the you that you were intended to be, the you that is more than you thought was possible. The you that is happier than imaginable, rooted in Jesus. The you that is unhindered and unashamed. The you that you have always wanted to be. Abandon yourself to God and allow the Holy Spirit to change what only He can. See yourself the way He sees you, complete and beautiful and loved. The *new you* is the *true you*, and He is taking you to the other side!

Stronger

I often share inside jokes with myself and if no one else thinks I'm funny, I at least know I'll laugh at my jokes. I'm not exactly sure why, but sometimes I'll find myself speaking to myself in what sounds like Chinese proverbs from a fortune cookie. Well, it happened recently while swimming. While I was on a lap, I wanted to stop right there in the middle of the pool. My heart was beating fast, I felt like I had no more strength and I didn't know how I could make it all the way to the other end of the pool, when I had the thought, "You don't know strength until you know and conquer weakness." That was all the motivation I needed to push myself to finish the lap.

Likewise, when I ran cross country, if I only ran the distance I was comfortable with, if I never pushed myself beyond my own limits and really broke a sweat, what growth could I have expected to take place?

When we feel like quitting the most but we don't, when we push ourselves to go another mile, we take ground and make progress. We become stronger when we feel the weakest, yet we refuse to give up and we don't quit. Feelings will come and go, but we can learn to live beyond them, trusting and finding strength in our Father who loves us with an unchanging love.

It's easy to have joy, stay motivated, and love people when it's comfortable. However, if we keep going when we feel the weakest and the most inadequate, refusing to allow those discouraging thoughts and feelings to control us, we will tap into a grace and strength that is beyond ourselves. This is how we take ground spiritually. This is how we grow and move forward. We were designed to live this life refreshed with an inner strength that is beyond ourselves, energized, stabilized, propelled by an infusion of grace, knowing that God loves us and He is on our side.

"Be strong (strengthened inwardly) in the grace (spiritual blessing) that is [to be found only] in Christ Jesus."

2 Timothy 2:1

"Be strong in the Lord [be empowered through your union with Him]; draw your strength from Him [that strength which His boundless might provides]."

Ephesians 6:10

When you feel weak and think you have had enough, remember that, as Brother Jerry Savelle puts it, "You can take anything the devil can dish out!" Smith Wigglesworth puts it this way: "You are 1,000 times bigger on the inside than you are on the outside." The Greater One lives in you and He will strengthen you every step of the way. When you feel like you don't know what to do, just keep putting one foot in front of the other. Just keep believing God and take another step. Let the weak say, "I am strong!" You are strong in Jesus and He will take you to the other side!

Dare to Dream

When the LORD turned again the captivity of Zion, we were like them that dream. Then was our mouth filled with laughter, and our tongue with singing: then said they among the heathen, The LORD hath done great things for them. The LORD hath done great things for us; whereof we are glad.

Psalm 126:1–3

Let your soul dance with fresh vision for your life. Dream with your Father who loves you endlessly as you declare that the Lord has done great things for you!

Trust (lean on, rely on, and be confident) in the Lord and do good; so shall you dwell in the land and feed surely on His faithfulness, and truly you shall be fed.

Delight yourself also in the Lord, and He will give you the desires and secret petitions of your heart.

Commit your way to the Lord [roll and repose each care of your load on Him]; trust (lean on, rely on, and be confident) also in Him and He will bring it to pass.

Psalm 37:3–5

One day at a time, one step at a time, commit your way to the Lord. The Lord is a safe guardian of your dreams. He will bring them to pass. He will deposit desires within your heart and awaken you to your purpose. Spend time with the Creator and He will breathe fresh life to your dreams. Delight yourself in the Lord and He will give you the secret petitions of your heart.

The devil will try his best to paint pictures in your mind of every reason why you are not going to make it. However, like the apostle Paul, we can declare by faith that, "None of these things move me" (Acts 20:24). Do not allow the enemy to continue replaying the past in your mind. Do not get stuck looking at the things that are behind you that you cannot change. The pressure of the enemy does not have to move you! It is only a thin facade.

Therefore, since we do hold and engage in this ministry by the mercy of God [granting us favor, benefits, opportunities, and especially salvation], we do not get discouraged (spiritless and despondent with fear) or become faint with weariness and exhaustion. .... We are hedged in (pressed) on every side [troubled and oppressed in every way], but not cramped or crushed; we suffer embarrassments and are perplexed and unable to find a way out, but not driven to despair; we are pursued (persecuted and hard driven), but not deserted [to stand alone]; we are struck down to the ground, but never struck out and destroyed.

2 Corinthians 4:1, 8–9

The things that we are facing are only "light, momentary afflictions" compared to the glory God has reserved and waiting for us. Nothing that is behind you can compare to what is ahead of you. These challenges are only temporary. You are going to make it. If you don't quit — you win!

You have a guaranteed victory as long as you do not give up. My mom always says, "When the devil pushes us, we just have to push back! Stand your ground and refuse to back down!"

Laugh in the face of hardships, laugh at the things of your past that try to taunt you. You are not who your past says that you are. Be bold enough to know that your God is greater than anything that has happened behind you. I dare you to believe that! Allow God's limitless love to mold your identity and shape the way you see yourself.

God is doing a new thing in your life and He wants you to dream with Him like never before. Nothing is impossible! There is no dream that is too big. Your Father wants you to get your hopes way up there, as high as they will go so He can not only match that expectation, but He will do superabundantly above and beyond anything you could dare to hope, dream, or imagine!

CHAPTER 18

NO LIVING AMONG THE DEAD

B y far, the darkest moment in the history of mankind was the crucifixion of Jesus Christ. In the middle of the day, darkness literally engulfed the entire planet as our innocent Savior, the spotless Son of God, hung on the cross. Jesus cried out with a loud voice, releasing His spirit and at once, the veil of the temple was torn in two from top to bottom as the earth violently shook and the rocks were split in half.

With their hopes shattered, everyone who had set their trust upon Jesus did not know which way to turn. They were drowning in sorrow, confusion, and fear wondering how they could pick up the broken pieces of their lives. In their eyes, it was all over. "I've followed Jesus for years; I have given up everything, and all for what? He's dead now. Everything I lived for is upside down. Where will my life go from here?"

However, when it looked like it was too late, it was not over in the eyes of God. When it felt like all was lost, He had a plan to change everything in an instant.

If God could turn what appeared to be the darkest, most hopeless moment in history into the most glorious demonstration of triumph, rest assured He can transform any mess in your life into victory!

Three days after Jesus was crucified on the cross, some of His followers went to the tomb. To their utter shock, the women found the stone rolled away and the tomb empty. They were unable to find Jesus' body anywhere, when two angels appeared and asked them this important question: "Why are you looking for the living among the dead?" (Luke 24:5).

What a powerful question! We need to ask ourselves that very same thing. The devil wants us to hold on to a distorted perception of ourselves by getting us to look at our past. However, there is no life behind you. Holding on to your past is holding on to death. According to the Bible, being carnally minded and thinking about the negative things that are behind you actually work death in your soul. In other words, if your past is alive in your soul, you are not living fully alive.

After the angels asked that vital question, they continued by telling the women, "He is not here, but He is risen." In the same manner, you are not there, you are risen! You are not found in the pain of your past; that brokenness has no bearing on your soul. Your worth is not found in your failures, you are not the mistakes you have made. Your present and your future are not dictated by your past. Your identity is not tied up in the way others have treated you. You are not there, stuck in that old, dead depression, unforgiveness, or intimidation. You are risen to a new way of life.

Luke 24:8-9 says that as the women "remembered His words," they immediately left the tomb. I love that! What was the very first thing that the women did after they remembered the words of Jesus? They left the place of death! Let that sink in. The moment you remember what Jesus has told you about yourself and your life, you leave that place of soul death. As you remember what He has said about you and the identity you have in Him, realize that you will not be remembered for that. Leave death and enter into life. Forget the things that are behind you and press forward to the things that are ahead.

According to Colossians 3:16, it is vital to allow the word of Christ to have its home in our hearts and minds and to dwell in us richly. When the past dwells in our soul, we dwell in death. However, when the Word of God dwells in us, we dwell in life. Out with the old and in with the new! Out with soul torment and bondage and in with freedom. Out with death, in with life and peace.

When you remember what Jesus has said about you, you won't go on looking for your identity among the dead things that are behind you. The devil will no longer to be able to dig up dirt from your past to show you who you are, because your true identity is found in Jesus:

> And you [He made alive], when you were dead (slain) by [your] trespasses and sins . . . But God—so rich is He in His mercy! Because of and in order to satisfy the great and wonderful and intense love with which He loved us, even when we were dead (slain) by [our own] shortcomings and trespasses, He made us alive together in fellowship and in union with Christ; [He gave us the very life of Christ Himself, the same new life with which He quickened Him, for] it is by grace (His favor and mercy which you did not deserve) that you are saved (delivered from judgment and made partakers of Christ's salvation). And He raised us up together with Him and made us sit down together [giving us joint seating with Him] in the

heavenly sphere [by our virtue of our being] in Christ Jesus (the Messiah, the Anointed One).

Ephesians 2:1,4–6

Unending love was God's driving force behind it all. According to Ephesians 2:7, "He did this that He might clearly demonstrate throughout the ages to come the immeasurable (limitless, surpassing) riches of His free grace (His unmerited favor) in [His] kindness and goodness of heart toward us in Christ Jesus."

I love the truth that Matthew 28:7 reveals: "He has risen from the dead, and behold, He is going before you ." Death could not hold our Redeemer down, and because He is risen, you are risen to a completely new life and new quality of living. Life does not have to be the way it has always been. Things can be better than you ever thought possible all because Jesus is risen and you are alive in Him, seated in the place of victory.

Jesus has gone before you and prepared the way, so don't be afraid to walk on in and take the land. Possess what belongs to you and enjoy the life that has been given to you! Let's be people who remember the words of Jesus and immediately leave the graveyard of our old identity and dead soul ties. Just like the angels said, "He is risen, He is not here," you are risen, you are not there. You will not find yourself in your past. No more looking for the living among the dead. In my heart, I hear Jesus saying, "I've already set the captives free. Don't go on living like a dead man when I have already made you alive. I have made you new. I have taken you out of the bondage of that prison cell into freedom."

Only Believe

A new day dawned for us the moment Jesus busted out of the grave. He conquered hell, death, and the grave. The victory

He won, He won for us. I love what Jesus said in John 20:17, "I am ascending to My Father and to your Father, and to My God, and your God." What freedom and what love! Right when everything looked like it was falling apart, in an instant, all hopelessness was swallowed up by the glory of God. Jesus' resurrection proves that nothing is impossible with God.

The words that Jesus spoke in John 20:27 ring in my heart. Even after He was raised from the dead and was seen in the flesh by His disciples, He still had to encourage them to "be not faithless, but believing" (KJV). The Amplified Version puts it this way, "Stop your unbelief and believe!" He's saying the same thing to you today. It is time to rise up and believe that nothing is impossible! Believe that God can restore your soul, heal your heart, and turn this around for your good. Let's obey Jesus because He knows the way of victory.

Jesus went on to say in John 20:29, "Blessed are they that have not seen, and yet have believed" (KJV). The word "blessed" is often expounded as happy. Happy is the person who believes without seeing. That means you don't have to see it yet to believe it. You don't have to know how God is going to turn that mess in your life into something glorious to know and rest assured that He will. The believing life is the happy life because it is the life that God can touch and transform.

When Jesus' mother Mary first heard the plan of God for her life — that she would become pregnant and give birth to our Savior — the angel said to her, "For with God nothing is ever impossible and no word from God shall be without power or impossible of fulfillment" (Luke 1:37). Within that moment, Mary chose to believe that nothing is impossible. She responded, "Let it be done to me according to what you have said" (Luke 1:38). What beautiful belief! Luke 1:45 says, "And blessed is she that believed: for there shall be a performance of those things which were told her from the Lord" (KJV). The Amplified version puts it like this, "And blessed (happy, to be envied) is she who believed that there would be a fulfillment of the things that were told her from the Lord." Happy is she who believes that God will complete what He has started in her life and bring to pass the dreams He has placed within her heart!

Ephesians 3:20 and 21 says, "Now to Him Who, by (in consequence of) the [action of His] power that is at work within us, is able to [carry out His purpose and] do superabundantly, far over and above all that we [dare] ask or think [infinitely beyond our highest prayers, desires, thoughts, hopes, or dreams] — to Him be glory." Don't live small. No more limited thinking. God can do so much more than what you have seen! Your believing unleashes the power that is within you and takes you into the realm of impossibilities. Your believing causes the new thing God has planned to take place in your life. Dream big and God will do bigger. Expect more and God will surpass it all. God has ways to turn your life around that have never even crossed your mind.

As the women were on their way to Jesus' tomb, they wondered, "Who will roll away the stone from the door of the tomb for us?" (Mark 16:3). Within their limited thinking, they had no idea how they would roll away that gigantic stone. Their small expectations left them hoping that they could find men who were strong enough to move it, but God had a plan that never crossed their minds! The women didn't need to worry about figuring out how to move the stone because the moment they arrived, they saw that the tomb was already busted wide open. They thought all they were going to do was care for a deceased body, however, they discovered that Jesus was alive and well and had gone before them!

We don't have to live under the burden of trying to figure out our lives in our small thinking. God has gone ahead of us and prepared victory in bigger and more glorious than we have dared to dream. In an instant, His glory can shatter the grave of shame and loose you from that dead life. Believe that you will see God's goodness rewrite the story of your life. The same Spirit that raised Jesus from the dead can cause dead things to come to life; He can cause dreams that have laid dormant and turned into disappointments, to come to life and turn into realities. It's never too late! After Lazarus had already been in the grave for four days, Jesus boldly declared, "If you believe, you will see the glory of God." Then He said with a loud voice, "Lazarus, come forth." John 11:44 says, "And he that was dead came forth, bound hand and foot with graveclothes: and his face was bound about with a napkin. Jesus saith unto them, Loose him and let him go" (KJV).

Today, Jesus is looking at you and saying, "Come forth! Go forward into the new! Be loosed and let it go!" It is time to leave the place of the dead. Be loosed from the soul ties of your past. Quit lugging around that death; let it go and let yourself go forward.

Remember, according to Romans 8:28, God is able to turn this around for your good. That doesn't mean that God brings bad things — not at all! Rather, it means that when you go through bad things, God is so much greater than it all that even when you face something negative, God is going to turn that negative around for a positive. He is far greater than the past and greater than anything devil has tried to use to hold you down. It is time to know that Jesus is going to work things out for you. It doesn't matter what comes your way, the Greater One lives in you, so all things are possible to him who believes.

First Corinthians 2:8 reveals that none of the rulers of this world expected the story of the cross to end the way it did: "None of the princes of this world knew, for had they known it, they would not have crucified the Lord of glory" (KJV). No one who crucified Jesus dared to imagine that three days later, He would conquer the grave and rise victorious over death. Satan thought he had won. He thought it was all over. However, right when the devil thought he had Jesus right where he wanted Him, our Deliverer shattered death and stripped Satan of his power. And we were raised with Him! Now many have been born again into the family of God and seated in victory. Satan had no idea how painfully and utterly he was going to lose.

Likewise, had the devil known how powerfully God was going to turn around that shame in your life, he never would have messed with you. Had he known that you weren't going to just roll over, play dead, and quit, he never would have attempted to keep you bound. Right when the devil thinks he has you beat, get ready, because our God is a God of suddenlies! Your life will not just be as good as it once was, it will be better than anything you could imagine. The devil hoped he could paralyze you with your past, but God has a plan to turn that thing around and propel you forward!

CHAPTER 19

VISION

A t a time in my life when I felt like I had nothing to live for and no reason to go on, I began devouring Terri Savelle Foy's messages like candy, as she taught me how to dream again. I thank God for Terri. The messages God gave her were the light at the end of my tunnel and were the very thing that saved my life. I discovered that the one thing you need when you think it's over is vision. She makes the point that if you don't have anything to look forward to, you will always return to your past. Just like Lot's wife, you can lose your future by looking back.

Proverbs 29:18 says, "Where there is no vision, the people perish" (KJV). Without vision, we exist on the outside and die on the inside. Purpose breeds vision and vision gives way to new life. Get alone with the God who created you on purpose with a purpose and He will cause your heart to soar with fresh vision. Dream with your Creator, remembering that all things are possible.

A major part in God turning all things around for your good is Him empowering you to do new things, things you never would have dreamed would be possible. If we want a new life full of greater victories and greater joy, we have to do something new. We need to dare to believe God and dare to make a change.

God can use you right where you are, even as He takes you to where you want to be. He will use you to be the encouragement that others around you need. Your life will be an example to others of the limitless grace and faithfulness of God. You can never go too far or mess up so much that God cannot use you. You will reach people in a way that no one else on the face of the planet can. God will use the personality, the talents, and the dreams He has given you to make a difference in this world. You will not be remembered for what is behind you.

Lately, I've been getting rid of a lot of old clothes. In doing so, I am actually enlarging my closet and making room for new things. When you get rid of the devil's old way of thinking, you make room for the new. Out with the old and in with the new! It's time to get rid of those old thoughts, that old, depressed identity of rejection, that old shame, because Jesus came to make all things brand new. Securing the freedom that Jesus has for us begins with our thinking. That is why the Bible says we must be transformed by the renewing of our minds. Think a new way and enjoy a new quality of life. Be refreshed and renewed with the Word of God and make room for that new thing that is breaking forth in your life.

If you want that new thing, think a new way! Open up your mouth and shut the door to the devil. Don't look at where you are, look at where you are going. Don't stay where you are, go forward. When it looks and feels like all hope is gone, against hope, believe. Keep believing, keep speaking, and keep putting one foot in front of the other. When you don't know how you are going to make it, go forward. When you don't know how God is going to work this one out, go forward. When it feels like your past is trying to pull you back, go forward. Miracles are in front of you — not behind you — so go forward. Whatever He says to you, do it. Go forward. He makes a way through the sea and a path through the mighty waters. Take the next step and He will take you all the way to the other side!

Years from now, you will look back and give God thanks for how He beautifully redeemed your life from destruction, took you out of the pit and placed you in His kingdom, opened the prison door and set you free to be a blessing to this world. Go ahead and just give Him thanks now for what He is doing and will do. See it ahead of time and praise Him for it now. Increase your capacity to believe God and dream like never before.

> Yet we have the same spirit of faith as he had who wrote, I have believed, and therefore have I spoken. We too believe, and therefore we speak, . . . For our light, momentary affliction (this slight distress of the passing hour) is ever more and more abundantly preparing and producing and achieving for us an everlasting weight of glory [beyond all measure, excessively surpassing all comparisons and all calculations, a vast and transcendent glory and blessedness never to cease!], since we consider and look not to the things that are seen but to the things that are unseen; for the things that are visible are temporal (brief and fleeting), but the things that are invisible are deathless and everlasting.
>
> 2 Corinthians 4:13, 17–18

What is it that enabled Paul to say in 2 Corinthians 4:8 and 9, "We are troubled on every side, yet not distressed; . . . cast down but not destroyed" (KJV)? How could he declare he would not give up and would not become discouraged? Because of what he chose to look at. If he just opened his eyes, he would see defeat all around him. But he chose to look at what was not seen. Don't give up over something that is only temporal, which means it is subject to change. Like Paul, no matter what comes against you, just declare, "None of these things move me!"

Give God thanks for the dreams He has deposited within your heart. He never gives a dream without knowing exactly how He will bring it to pass in your life! Trust in the Lord, lean not to your own understanding, and He will bring every secret petition in your heart to pass. The steps of a good man are ordered by the Lord and He delights in every detail of your life. Though you may be cast down, though you may fall seven times, you shall arise.

A Vision for Others

During the hardest time of my life, I went to Honduras on a missions trip. To be honest, it was something I had no desire to do at the time, but I did it to get my eyes off of myself. By God's great grace and mercy, He used me to preach at my first evangelistic and healing crusade. It was there on the mission field, as I finally put myself to the side, that I realized God still loves me and He still wants to use me to help others.

That fact forever changed my life, and I was revitalized with fresh vision. Maybe: I learned to dream again. No matter what my past tried to say to limit me, I realized there were still people for me to reach and my future was still shining bright. As I was strengthened by the Word of God, which is the incorruptible seed that produces incorruptible results, I decided to just start right where I was and make every day count. I made daily goals, starting with simply spending time with God. While doing so, I began to dream of the mission field, of helping people from all walks of life be set free from shame. I had a reason to live again. My eyes were no longer on myself.

Vision will carry you through the hardest of times. When you have something you are looking at, you can move forward towards it. The more time we spend with God, the more we realize how precious and irreplaceable we are to Him. Then we realize that every other person on the face of the planet is just as valuable. When we become all about God, we become all about others. Our lives become more satisfying when we determine to love like never before and live to be a blessing to those around us.

According to 2 Timothy 3, one of the greatest temptations for God's people in the last days will be to become self-centered, focusing on "me" — my pain, what I'm going through — to the point that we forget about everyone else. However, by becoming so self-centered, we actually separate ourselves from our full healing. When we allow God's love and healing power to flow out of us to help someone else, we receive of that same fullness in an even greater way.

God wants you to begin to dream again about how He can use you to make a difference and bring freedom to others. Such indescribable joy comes when we give of ourselves to be used by God. Live to love and you will love life. There is too much of a difference for you to make, too many people for you to help for you to get stuck here!

Make it your determined purpose each and every day to know God more. Trust Him with your future. Trust Him with your dreams. Trust Him that the best days of your life are ahead of you and not behind you. Trust God enough to know that He can do beyond what you had before and beyond what you have ever imagined. Terri Savelle Foy says, "When what you see on the inside is more real than what you see on the outside, what you see on the outside will change! Get a vision for your life, even if it is just starting with five simple things. . . . The secret to your future is hidden in your daily routine."

I have come to realize the value of a single step. Incorporating just one small step into your daily routine can completely transform your life when you remain consistent. Take a step today, there is nothing too small. Read your Bible. Pray in the spirit to build up inner strength. Giving God thanks daily can be that one step that catapults you into the new thing God is wanting to do in your life.

Terri says, "We will never leave where we are until we see where we would rather be." Get a picture of where you know God wants to take your life and keep it before your eyes. Write the vision out. Speak it and give God thanks every day. I am fully convinced that thanking God for the fulfillment of your dreams before you see or feel that anything has changed is the sure way to experience the biggest breakthrough in your life. A person whose soul is so anchored in the Finisher of their faith, who refuses to let any circumstance rob his or her joy, who remains steadfast and confident in the midst of the greatest storms, declaring, "I know that my God works out ALL things together for my good" — the devil CANNOT defeat a person like that! That's the type of person I am determined to be and that's the type of person you are. Victory is inevitable for a man or woman like you!

A New Outlook

Let these words be ingrained in your spirit: All things are not possible for all people; *only for those who believe*. God wants to turn this around for your good, but He works with your faith. Faith works by love and faith comes by hearing the word of God. It is easy to trust someone when you know they love you, that they've got your back, and that they will never leave you. Well, God loves you with everything that He is. He will never stop believing in you and He isn't going anywhere. Believing God is simply a by-product of knowing how much He cares for you.

Your attitude has everything to do with your outcome. Whenever something comes your way, take notice of your attitude because that will let you know what you are truly believing and focusing on. If you don't like your attitude, then change your focus! Don't major on what the devil is doing; magnify God and focus on how He is turning the tide!

Proverbs 4:23 says, "Guard your heart above all else, for it determines the course of your life" (NLT). Jerry Savelle refers to faith and joy as "life-giving forces." These life-giving forces reside in your heart. They grow by feeding on the Word and when given place to, they activate and release the hand of God to work on your behalf. You cannot stay in the same place and you cannot live bound when you give place to joy. A joyful attitude reflects confident expectation in God. God works with expectation. That is faith! He will take your expectation and not only meet it, but far exceed it.

The devil has no defense against someone who refuses to let go of their joy. Can you imagine how irritated and hopeless that makes the devil feel when he gives all he's got to try to discourage you, and you just go on rejoicing, singing, and shouting, "This greater difficulty just means I'm gonna have a greater breakthrough!" When nothing can keep you down, then nothing can defeat you.

> Don't be intimidated in any way by your enemies. This will be a sign to them that they are going to be destroyed, but that you are going to be saved, even by God himself.
>
> **Philippians 1:28 NLT**

> For I know that as . . . the Spirit of Jesus Christ helps me, this will lead to my deliverance.
>
> **Philippians 1:19 NLT**

Rejoice in the Lord always [delight, gladden yourselves in Him]; again I say, Rejoice!

Philippians 4:4

Celebrate God all day, every day.

Philippians 4:4 MSG

Don't let anything the adversary does intimidate you; instead, celebrate God all day long! Refuse to live intimidated by your past and afraid of your future. Satan does not stand a chance to rob you of your joy if you are celebrating God all day long. In fact, any and all adversity can be overcome by the power of joy. That's exactly why the devil will try to steal your joy from you.

The Bible says we are not to be ignorant of the devil's devices. Imagine how easy a victory in any sport would be if your team knew exactly what plays the opposing team planned to make. That knowledge would arm you with a great advantage. Well, you do have that kind of advantage over Satan because he always uses the same tactics. He will try to get you to obsess over the past. He wants you to get stuck in the chains of shame so that your life will be swallowed up by regret, never to progress. However, a person who refuses to let any contradictory circumstances keep him from believing what the word says is a person the devil cannot defeat. Thanking God ahead of time for what He has promised to do in your life according to what He has said in His Word will keep you full of joy. Stay thankful and you will stay happy.

Doubt bites us in the butt. A doubter never wins. Doubt robs us of our joy and breeds self-pity and unthankfulness. Doubt will keep you stuck feeling sorry for yourself. Our attitude is like a magnet. An attitude that reflects belief in God makes way for more and more thankfulness, and a thankful person never does without. Doubt and you will do without. Believe and you'll receive.

Your outlook has everything to do with your outcome. Maintain your future by maintaining your joy. Keep dreaming. Keep believing. Keep speaking. Keep standing. You will win as long as you do not quit. Run with the vision that God has given you and have enough tenacity to make up your mind ahead of time that come hell or high water, you will not quit. Stick it out. Don't throw away your confidence. Stick with God's plan and you will see the promised completion.

This is the life of faith. We are not of those who draw back and shrink in fear. We are the believing ones (Hebrews 10:39)! We step out in faith and we see miracles. Keep seeing it now in your heart and you will see it then in your life. Speak it now and you will live it then. Give thanks now and you will always win!

Psalm 118:15 says, "Hear the shouts, hear the triumph songs in the camp of the saved? The hand of GOD has turned the tide!" (MSG). God is turning the tide in your life! The devil's intended purpose will not come to pass. His plans have backfired and God of the Great Turnaround has turned the tide in your favor! He makes ALL things new, He works ALL things together for your good, and He ALWAYS causes you to triumph. ALL things are possible for those believe. Sounds to me like you have a whole lot of rejoicing to do. One thing I know for sure, where there's a lot of joy and rejoicing, there's a lot of victories!

Time for the New

God is taking you to places you've never been before. You are loosed! You are free to love yourself, free to dream and free to move forward! It is not too late for you. All things are possible for those who believe. This is not the end. Satan will not have the final say in your life. Keep believing, keep dreaming, keep your joy and you will see God turn all things around for your good. You will finish your course with joy. You will make a difference in this world. You will see the promised completion. You will be remembered for being who God has created you to be and doing what He has placed in your heart.

God loves you. He always has and He always will. Nothing you have ever done or ever will do has the power to change His mind about you. He has great plans and huge dreams for your life. Dream with God. Love yourself. You are not the mistakes you have made and you are not what other people have done to you. When your Father God sees you, He sees the child He has always wanted and He has beautiful plans for you. He is holding out a fresh start to you at this very moment. Believe God. Rest in His unchanging love for you. Find your identity in His open arms.

Quit going over old history. God is doing a NEW thing in your life and it has already begun! You have so much to live for, there is no need to look back. Your greatest days are ahead. With all that is within me, I pray that you are daily encouraged and strengthened by the Holy Spirit to say, "But one thing I do [it is my one aspiration]: forgetting what lies behind and straining forward to what lies ahead, I press on" (Philippians 3:13-14). The God's Word translation puts it this way, "This is what I do: I don't look back, I lengthen my stride, and I run straight toward the goal to win the prize that God's heavenly call offers in Christ Jesus."

Let it go and GO FORWARD! Remember, miracles are in front of you, not behind you. Keep putting one foot in front of the other and keep going forward because you are standing right on the brink of your biggest breakthrough. You are no longer paralyzed by your past but propelled into your God-given future. Your Father has not left you stuck in the dust of shame, but He has made all things new and redeemed your life from destruction. Go forward. This is your time!

The Message paraphrase of Amos 9:13 and14 announces, "'Yes indeed, it won't be long now.' GOD's Decree. 'Things are going to happen so fast your head will swim, one thing fast on the heels of the other. You won't be able to keep up. Everything will be happening at once—and everywhere you look, blessings!'"

This is your great year of breaking loose and the time of your great turnaround — your season of change. I believe you will look back on this specific year and rejoice that, without a doubt, this was the turning point, where everything became different. God can do more in this one year of your life then has taken place in the past five years combined because He is so much greater than your past. When God works, who or what can hinder or reverse it? Everywhere you look you will see restoration and freedom!

Live in the freedom of His love. Dream new, big dreams and then watch God surpass anything you dare to imagine. As Habakkuk 2:2 says, "And the Lord answered me, and said, Write the vision, and make it plain upon tables, that he may run that readeth it" (KJV). Dream like never before, write the vision, and run with everything within you. Things will take place in your life at an accelerated speed if you press in and take the limits off of your thinking. Enlarge the place of your tent — the new is bursting through! Believe and nothing will be impossible. God is the giver of those dreams within you and He is the One who will bring them to pass. He deposited those dreams within you on purpose and they will take place.

Don't go one more day living as a prisoner of your past. Do not continue to look at yourself as damaged goods. That is not who you are. You are loved. When God looks at you, He sees worth and purpose. See yourself the same way. Hear Him shouting to you, "You will not be remembered for that! You will not be remembered for that! You will not be remembered for that!"

The prison door has been flung open wide and shame no longer has power over you. Your Father God loves you. He has redeemed you and He is calling you by name. You are His. You belong. You have a future that is brighter than anything you could dare to dream. So live free, full and go forward with your head lifted high and shoulders back, knowing that God is within you, so you cannot fail. He is working all things for your good. Your best days are in front of you and the new has already begun. You are loved, you can love yourself, and you can move forward.

When God looks at you, He sees worth and purpose. See yourself the same way. He has redeemed you and He is calling you by name. You are His. You belong. You have a future that is brighter than anything you could dare to dream. So live free, full and go forward with your head lifted high and shoulders back, knowing that God is within you, so you cannot fail. He is working all things for your good. Your best days are in front of you and the new has already begun.

You, my friend, will NOT be remembered for that.

ABOUT THE AUTHOR

 Olivia Moore is a passionate lover of God and people. Her transparent, relatable teaching style refreshes and energizes others to act on God's Word and to live the adventurous, heart-satisfying life God has designed them to live.

Growing up in a ministry family, Olivia has had the joy of knowing Jesus her entire life. At the age of 15, she stepped into ministry and has been sharing the gospel around the world ever since. Olivia graduated from Rhema Bible Training College in 2011 and was ordained in 2014, through Dr. Jerry Savelle's Heritage of Faith Christian Center.

Known as a "fireball preacher with a smile," her purpose is simply knowing Jesus and making Him known. Olivia desires to see this world set on fire by the same love that has given her life. She helps others from all walks of life experience freedom from their past, joy in their present, and vision for their future.

Olivia lives in Miami, Florida. Along with being a traveling evangelist, she serves on the ministerial staff of the church her grandparents founded and parents pastor, Words of Life.

Visit oliviamoore.org for messages, vlog posts, itinerary, and more!

PRAYER OF SALVATION

God loves you—no matter who you are, no matter what your past. God loves you so much that He gave His one and only begotten Son for you. The Bible tells us that "...whoever believes in Him shall not perish but have eternal life" (John 3:16 NIV). Jesus laid down His life and rose again so that we could spend eternity with Him in heaven and experience His absolute best on earth. If you would like to receive Jesus into your life, say the following prayer out loud and mean it from your heart.

Heavenly Father, I come to You admitting that I am a sinner. Right now, I choose to turn away from sin, and I ask You to cleanse me of all unrighteousness. I believe that Your Son, Jesus, died on the cross to take away my sins. I also believe that He rose again from the dead so that I might be forgiven of my sins and made righteous through faith in Him. I call upon the name of Jesus Christ to be the Savior and Lord of my life. Jesus, I choose to follow You and ask that You fill me with the power of the Holy Spirit. I declare that right now I am a child of God. I am free from sin and full of the right-eousness of God. I am saved in Jesus' name. Amen.

If you prayed this prayer to receive Jesus Christ as your Savior for the first time, please contact us on the Web at **www.harrisonhouse.com** to receive a free book.

Or you may write to us at
Harrison House • P.O. Box 35035 • Tulsa, Oklahoma 74153

The Harrison House Vision

Proclaiming the truth and the power

Of the Gospel of Jesus Christ

With excellence;

Challenging Christians to

Live victoriously,

Grow spiritually,

Know God intimately.

Fast. Easy. Convenient.

For the latest Harrison House product information and author news, look no further than your computer. All the details on our powerful, life-changing products are just a click away. New releases, e-mail subscriptions, testimonies, monthly specials — find it all in one place. Visit **harrison**house.com today!

harrisonhouse.com